LANGUAGE AND LITERACY

Dorothy S. Strickland, FOUND
Celia Genishi and Donna E. Alverma

ADVISORY BOARD: Richard Allington, Kathryn Au, Bernice Cull
Carole Edelsky, Shirley Brice Heath, Connie Juel, S

MW01014334

(continued)

For volumes in the NCRLL Collection (edited by JoBeth Allen and Donna E. Alvermann) and the Practitioners Bookshelf Series (edited by
Celia Genishi and Donna E. Alvermann), please visit www.tcpress.com.

"Trust Me! I Can Read"

Building from Strengths in the High School English Classroom

Sally Lamping
Dean Woodring Blase

Foreword by Cathy Fleischer

Teachers College
Columbia University
New York and London

Published by Teachers College Press, 1234 Amsterdam Avenue, New York, NY 10027

Library of Congress Cataloging-in-Publication Data

Lamping, Sally.
  Trust me! I can read : building from strengths in the high school English classroom / Sally
    Lamping, Dean Woodring Blase ; Foreword by Cathy Fleischer.
      pages cm. — (Language and literacy series)
  ISBN 978-0-8077-5327-9 (pbk. : alk. paper)
    1. Reading (Secondary)—United States. 2. Motivation in education—United States. I. Blase,
  Dean Woodring. II. Title.
  LB1632.L338 2012
  428.4071'2—dc23   2012005150

ISBN 978-0-8077-5327-9 (paper)

Printed on acid-free paper
Manufactured in the United States of America

19 18 17 16 15 14 13 12   8 7 6 5 4 3 2 1

Contents

Foreword

ISPEND A LOT of time these days—as I imagine you do, too—reading newspapers, blogs, legislative mandates, and other assorted materials that alternatively make me confused, incensed, and frustrated. Many voices are proclaiming very loudly that schools are failing, that too many teachers are incompetent, and that the answers to the challenges of education lie in increased standardization of curriculum and assessment. In my best moments (and I admit, these are few and far between these days), I want to believe these loud voices care as deeply about kids and their successes as I do—as all the teachers I work with do—but that our beliefs about how to get there are just different. In my worst moments, I am just plain terrified—terrified about the future of education, about the "lost generation" of students I fear will come out of this reign, about the status of teachers. I wonder how the many amazing teachers I know will be able to continue to create the kinds of special learning environments they do if they are no longer given the freedom to know their students and to put into practice effective, research-based strategies.

Yet, as Chiseri-Strater and Sunstein (2006) remind us, "We need to make our voices speak through the fire and invite the noisy public to listen" (p. xvi). They imagine a cadre of teachers speaking out about the good work that goes on in so many schools and classrooms. They challenge teachers to take on the mantle of classroom researcher, systematically studying what works in their classrooms and having the courage to share that work with others. Sally Lamping and Dean Woodring Blase are two teachers who have answered that challenge in a particularly thoughtful way. In *"Trust Me! I Can Read,"* they situate their writing in their own classroom experiences, offering us portraits of students and curricula that do work—and, most important, that work in ways that are respectful of both students and teachers.

That respect comes through in the question that drives their inquiry: How can English teachers empower their students to become knowledgeable and curious lifelong learners rather than merely skilled test takers? They argue that in order to do so, we need to recognize that the essence of teaching English is more than creating a generation of students who *can* read—but rather a generation of students who *do* read. Building upon the work of Steven Wolk (2009) when he writes, "While a nation of workers requires a country that *can* read, a democracy requires people that *do* read, read widely, and think and act in response to their reading" (p. 665), Lamping and Blase suggest there are societal patterns at work that create students who *can* but who *don't*. They write compellingly about what teachers, as "stewards of [students'] literacy journeys," might actually do to break these patterns.

For Lamping and Blase, breaking the pervasive patterns begins with trust: trusting the students and trusting the literature. A pedagogy of trust means moving away from classroom practice that is informed by fear and toward practice that is based in knowledge, high expectations, and understanding of students—a message that is "contrary to the message district officials concerned with NCLB rankings often tell teachers: they cannot trust that students can read." But what would happen, they ask, "if teachers and schools defied this deficit assumption, and instead began with the possibility that what all students bring to classrooms and reading experiences will change the way teachers read or teach a novel forever?"

A wonderful question, I think, and one that they answer as the book continues. Situating their work in real classrooms, they give us portraits of how they have trusted themselves and their students and have, in turn, helped students come to see literature—and the role of reading—differently. Calling upon an "I Choose, You Choose" curriculum, they show us how students can move from reading teacher-assigned texts, to choosing books and reading together in groups, to self-selecting texts and reading independently—trusting that the students will engage with pieces of literature in critical and thoughtful ways if they trust in the power of the literature. Across the many examples they offer of how to put these ideas into practice, they always focus on how these experiences are not designed to test *if* students have read, but rather to help students use what they read to come to greater understandings of the world around them. And the student work they share demonstrates how well these approaches can work.

But, some may ask, what of tests and standardized curricula? Where do these realities fit into their schema? In the current climate, teachers cannot ignore the demands that these concerns place on them, and Lamping and Blase don't ignore them either. Rather, they put these tests in their place, arguing convincingly what many of us know is true: that students who become more engaged readers *will* do better on standardized tests. This is no small point, especially as we look for ways to save a generation of students who are increasingly pummeled by an approach to standardization that too often reduces the time and value placed on meaningful reading. Serious literature study is not the problem, they suggest; rather, "It is when we make reading a chore or outcome-based that students become disillusioned by books."

As I read this book, I found myself nodding my head and jotting notes to share with the preservice and practicing teachers with whom I work. But as

I thought about sharing the specific strategies that Lamping and Blase advocate, I realized that this book—while it is indeed filled with strategies and classroom examples—is not really about those things, or at least not about those alone. Instead, I think this is a book about reflective teacher practice, about beginning with the knowledge and beliefs thoughtful teachers have developed and searching for answers about how to teach in ways that are congruent with those beliefs. In other words, Lamping and Blase never suggest their approaches to teaching should serve as models that others should adopt whole-scale. Rather, they emphasize that reflective teacher practice, reliant as it is on context and relationship, is at the heart of teacher change. And so throughout the book, they invite readers to reflect: In sections they call "Extend Your Thinking," they offer teachers a chance to think carefully about their own questions about teaching and to write and talk their way into considering what their next steps might be. For Lamping and Blase, teacher reflection is the most powerful tool we have to combat the atmosphere of fear that pervades teaching lives these days. When teachers understand the research that supports thoughtful ways of teaching and when they are able to take on the mantle of teacher researchers themselves, they are more able to "make [their] voices speak through the fire."

Will concerned educators be able to change the current wave of scripted curriculum and testing gone awry? I do not know. But I do know that when I read books like *"Trust Me! I Can Read"* and hear the passion of authors like Lamping and Blase, I come away more hopeful. And when I imagine teachers reading this book and taking the authors up on their heartfelt (and well-argued) plea to trust each other, to trust their students, and to become increasingly reflective about their own practice, I realize that all of our voices are needed to make a difference. I invite you to read this book with that sense of purpose: to listen to the wise words that Sally Lamping and Dean Blase offer us, to analyze what they've done in their own classrooms, and to make the kinds of changes in your own that will honor and respect the amazing students that you teach.

—Cathy Fleischer
Eastern Michigan University

References

Chiseri-Strater, E., & Sunstein, B. S. (2006). *What works? A practical guide for teacher research.* Portsmouth, NH: Heinmann.

Wolk, S. (2009). Reading for a better world: Teaching for social responsibility with young adult literature. *Journal of Adolescent and Adult Literacy, 52*(8), 664–673.

Acknowledgments

WE WOULD LIKE TO acknowledge all of our students, past, present, and future, who teach us to trust. We would also like to acknowledge our partners and families for their support. We thank our editors at Teachers College Press for their precise work and our colleagues at Wright State University and Harvard School of Education for their continuing dialogues. We would like to thank Michael Smyth for his incredible photographs. We would also like to add that all the student examples in this book are used with pseudonyms and great care has been taken to articulate these voices authentically. Last but not least, we would like to give special thanks to our former teaching colleagues, Carly Andrews and Lynda Kale, who have taught us so much.

Introduction
What Happened to High School Readers?

Hey Sally,

I am teaching at a local high school. I have 9th-grade college prep classes. I am only part time, so I have four classes a day and only one prep. It is about as country as it can get lol! I love it! I wish it was full time but other than that, I love it. I know that you really don't have to do anything for us anymore, but a lot of our cohort is really upset and depressed about their situations. As far as I know, Elizabeth moved to a different state, and she has a job and I have a part-time job, but other than that no one got a job. They are all getting really down. Could you possibly send everyone an encouraging email? I know that it would help. I know that you can't fix the problem, but I think hearing from you would be encouraging.

I miss being in your class. I wish that you could see my classroom! Everyone in this building has straight rows, teaches straight from a textbook, and has no posters or creativity at all. Then you walk into mine and my classroom is super colorful. I have the students in groups, and we have done all sorts of mini-projects already this year. It is great!

Thanks,
Heather

How DOES A NEW or seasoned teacher maintain resilience, empathy, and creativity in a troubled educational climate? In the email above, Heather exemplifies three outcomes of graduating from a teacher-education program focused on building trust through standards-based curricula in English classrooms. First, even though she has found work, she still feels a strong connection to her classmates from the program and wants to support them (empathy). Second, she is not afraid to rely on her mentors, even though she has since graduated from their classes (connectedness). The third outcome is that she is confident as a new teacher in a rigid educational climate (resilience). In her teacher-education program, she saw a trust-based curriculum at work, and, because of her experience, she feels supported in employing these practices in her own classroom—even though she is the only one in her school. As a result, her students are reaping the benefits by engaging with reading and writing on a variety of critical levels. Heather (and many others like her) knows the high school English classroom is a place of possibility and power.

Instead of working alone to *practice* reading comprehension, vocabulary development, and analysis through a series of computer-based activities, worksheets, and sample tests, students in Heather's classroom live their reading experiences by trying out their new understandings of texts in small reading communities, completing experiential projects that allow them to explore the implications of reading within the context of the larger world, and using technology to collaborate and share reading through social networking sites for readers (webpage development, character fan pages, and movie trailers for books).

Her students move around the classroom when they work, interacting with one another as readers and thinkers. They learn how to agree or disagree with an idea, not a person, and ground these opinions in text through student-led seminar. Most important, they trust their teacher because, all the while, she's working to provide them with focused feedback, strategies to organize their time and reading, parameters for classwork that are not punitive, and substantial opportunities to dialogue about books with her through conversations, journals, and projects.

Heather uses her reading curriculum to educate the whole child. In these activities, they are certainly learning what the testing culture wants them to learn (reading comprehension, vocabulary development, inference, summary, analysis), but they are also learning, through their interactions with texts and one another, how to be creative and critical thinkers, respectful individuals who are confident in their opinions, and empathetic readers and colleagues—all while developing trust in their growing curricular knowledge and building strong foundations for lifelong reading.

Heather is also a 1st-year teacher. Like many new teachers, Heather is still learning the expectations of her new school and striving to balance assessments, standards, and content within her classes. Because she's set up a classroom based on trust, however, she opens herself to ample opportunities for growth as a reader and teacher. By seeing her students as fellow readers, she invites a two-way dialogue that will expand her reading and teaching repertoire through her own reflective practice. When Heather first entered Sally's undergraduate Reading Workshop class, she described herself as a slow or nonreader. And yet she is now a teacher who has discovered a genuine and insatiable love of reading. As a result, she knows what it can offer her students: an opportunity to build relationships with literature that nurture critical minds and, equally, an opportunity to experience interconnectedness with each other. It is easy to surmise that Heather will continue to mentor these students long after they leave her classroom.

THE PEDAGOGY OF POVERTY

This book would serve no purpose if the preceding paragraphs were true in every high school classroom, regardless of context. Sadly, these types of interactions only seem to exist in some schools; in others, the high-stakes testing movement holds students and teachers hostage. Equally, the dismal job market that Heather describes can exacerbate the levels of teacher fear and compliance with test-prep practices in classrooms. The pedagogy of poverty that Martin Haberman (1991) described 20 years ago has grown exponentially with the high-stakes testing movement, particularly in low-income and urban schools. This type of teaching relies heavily on control (government, district, administrative), teacher directives, and student submission. In recent years, these pedagogies have evolved into a primary focus on standardized test preparation and the abilities of students to follow directions precisely. What this means for students and teachers in low-income and urban schools is devastating: "The overly directive, mind-numbing, mundane, useless, anti-intellectual acts that constitute teaching not only remain the coin of the realm but have become the gold standard" (Haberman, 2010, p. 45).

It is impossible to say that trust exists or even matters in pedagogies designed to produce quantifiable outcomes instead of dynamic individuals. High-stakes testing policies have systematically removed the human element from schooling, and too many educators have forgotten that for students to really and truly learn anything, they have to first trust that learning can happen. This book asks high school English teachers to subvert the dominant pedagogy of poverty and, instead, trust students as literate, cognitive beings.

No Child Left Behind

As veteran teachers, we believe that No Child Left Behind (NCLB) and the report that purportedly spawned it, *A Nation at Risk: The Imperative for Educational Reform* (National Commission on Excellence in Education, 1983), have done more to erode trust in the American public school system than any other single force. In reexamining *A Nation at Risk* nearly a quarter of a century later, we are struck by the overt message of fear in its opening rhetoric: "We have, in effect, been committing an act of unthinking, unilateral educational disarmament" (1983, p. 1). The discourse of the late-1960s culture wars has become the discourse of education. *A Nation at Risk* compounded this and publically and, most important, politically extended the education "war" into the 21st century. Although the report quickly and successfully led to early calls to action to improve education, it has had a lasting and detrimental effect on trust among various stakeholders (students, teachers, administrators, and parents) in American public schools. Efforts to implement NCLB have placed many teachers in a position of fearful compliance: they are afraid to stray from prescriptive test preparation methods laid out by administration.

NCLB has not only failed to deliver on the promises of *A Nation at Risk*, but it continues to erode classroom trust by using narrow forms of assessment to deem the success or failure of educational practices. With systems of mandated assessments and complicated algorithms for determining adequate yearly progress, NCLB can lead to often frightening consequences for students, teachers, schools, and districts. Everything teachers do must pay off in assessable outcomes or it is questioned. We have taught in this environment and have found productive ways to maintain accountability to NCLB while also addressing our students' need to be well educated. We believe that the methods we present in this book articulate how we established our trustworthiness as teachers and simultaneously modeled classrooms built on self-reliance, interdependence, and resilience.

Teaching Standards Versus Teaching Tests

Teachers who are masters of their content areas and use this mastery to promote engaging experiences in their classrooms are teaching the standards. Nevertheless, when the teaching methods appear to stray from test preparation, especially in "failing" schools, these teachers will be questioned.

We recently got a different email from Lisa, another 1st-year teacher. Lisa reported that she was asked, without warning, to defend her use of reading workshops to the administration in her building. Lisa's students were actively choosing books, reading in comfortable spots in the classroom, and talking quietly with their peers and teacher about their choices. Even though students were critically and thoughtfully exploring the standards, Lisa's methods were suddenly scrutinized because they veered from the prescriptive format seen in all the other classrooms at the school. When called to the office, she brought a sequence of studies citing the correlation between independent reading and test scores. She defended her practice and won, but the administration forced her to assess the students' reading journals. She felt this was a fair compromise in an effort to keep a practice that she knew would ultimately benefit her students. Because Lisa graduated from a program that stressed valid research-based pedagogy and gave her all the tools to defend this pedagogy, she defended her practice with confidence and ease. She proved what she already knew: her methods could raise the consciousness of readers in her classroom to a far more advanced level than test preparation ever could.

At a huge expense, teaching to the test has done little to increase test scores. The 2009 ACT report *The Condition of College Readiness* posits that only 53% of all members of the class of 2009 were ready for college-level reading upon graduation. Even more alarming is the enormous gap among races: A whopping 42 percentage points separates the least-prepared group (African American students) from the highest (White students) (p. 13–15). (Keep in mind, however, that ACT's reading standards only address five areas: main ideas and author's approach; supporting detail; sequential, comparative, and cause-effect relationships; meanings of words; and generalizations and conclusions [ACT, 2011]. Limiting student reading to what's embedded in the text and excluding the rich experience of reading itself is yet another symptom of the standards movement.) In addition, the Bill and Melinda Gates Foundation's recent (2010) study on Measures of Effective Teaching (MET) finds that "[teacher focus on] test preparation was among the weakest predictors of gains on the state tests" (p. 24). This is not only ironic, it's tragic.

REBUILDING TRUST

In 1956, Louise Rosenblatt wrote that high school literature teachers should strive to "help young people to discover the power of literature to enable us to experiment imaginatively with life" (1956, p. 70). At the center of this endeavor, we believe, must be a core foundation of trust; without it, students and teachers would be unable to take such personal risks with literature. As Parker Palmer (2007) writes, *"To teach is to create a space in which the community of truth is practiced"* (p. 92). He explains that such a community is neither teacher- nor student-focused but subject-centered. Unless schools first trust that both teachers and students bring assets into the literature classroom, we believe that it is impossible to place subject at the center.

Two conflicting paradigms heavily influenced our own careers as high school teachers: the student-centered curriculum, which advocates group work, student leadership and initiative, independence balanced with interdependence, dialogue, and inquiry-based models of learning; and the high-stakes testing movement, which advocates memorization, independent learning, and top-down methods of instruction. Although we began our practices steeped in Rosenblatt's reader-response theories, we went on to find the writing of Nancie Atwell (1998), who proved that such theories could translate into pedagogy in the reading workshop classroom. We soon understood the power of teacher research to reclaim and transform the English classroom. We entered our first classrooms at the beginning of the standards movement. Now, more than 15 years later, our work as educators is still immersed in the belief that "books do not simply happen to people. People also happen to books" (Rosenblatt, 1956, p. 66). In other words, we know from our experiences as teachers that what readers bring to a text and the way they interact with a text as a result cannot be ignored. Our belief that individual readers contribute to the meaning of books enlivened our work as English teachers. Our commitment to valuing each student's interaction with texts grew out of our experiences with the standards movement, our work in suburban and urban public high schools, our interactions with parents and administrators from a variety of backgrounds, and our brushes with censorship. It continues to inform our belief in the transformational power of a high school literature classroom in *any* context: it remains a place of possibility.

Instead of placing students and the content at the center of the classroom, test preparation practices promote a narrow relationship with literature: one based on teaching and getting the right answer. These are the dangers that arise when teachers allow governmental, district, and administrative pressures, along with personal fears, to get in the way of students engaging with literature. Richard Elmore (2004) proposes a definition of the "instructional core" as simply (and significantly) being "the relationship of the teacher and the student in the presence of content" (p. 291). Elmore turns us back to the shared space of content and relationships in successful schooling.

Maria Montessori (1948/1992) in *From Childhood to Adolescence* reminds us that our work with students should be age appropriate. She denotes specific traits of high school students that are radically different from their younger counterparts: "The chief symptom of adolescence is a state of expectation, a tendency toward creative work and a need for the strengthening of self-confidence" (p. 61). In a high school classroom, students need social opportunities to share their views of literature with one another, but they also need to develop the self-reliance to discover their own relationships with literature. This is true whether a classroom is heterogeneously grouped or separated by "ability." Students' need to connect with peers, teachers, and literature has nothing to do with how well they can read and write.

Rebuilding Trust in Teachers

Too often, teachers assume that their students can't read when the problem is that they won't read according to prescription. Jeanine, a teacher candidate, reported to us a story that exemplified the disconnection between what she had learned was good teaching practice and the extremes of prescriptive methods. The student-teaching video she shared with us revealed a remarkable classroom culture that resulted from these constraints. Jeanine's job was to play a cassette tape companion to the literature textbook, which provided an audio version of the story and directives about answering questions at the end of each selection. The students read along simultaneously in the literature textbooks. Per the audiotape's instructions, Jeanine pauseD the cassette and ask a few questions from the end of the textbook's chapter. She then moved on to play the tape again. This continued for the entire class.

In watching the video, the audience can see the students, especially those who were labeled as "failing," slowly sink into their seats, doodle on their papers, and pass notes to their neighbors. What went wrong here? Were the students deemed unteachable? Was the student teacher predetermined to be incompetent and not to be trusted to plan an actual lesson? When did the trust begin to disintegrate, or did it ever exist?

When we questioned Jeanine about what she would do differently if she were in charge, Jeanine noted that she would have trusted students to do the reading on their own (some days in class and some as part of homework) and then use class time to engage them with the literature by working individually, in pairs, or in groups. She believed that if she could engage them through dramatic role play; creative use of technology; small-group discussions and larger, student-led seminar; and through artistic responses that developed a reading and writing connection rather than use the textbook to do so, they might be more willing to do the reading assignments on their own. We can compare Jeanine's idea with Heather's experience implementing these methods in a rural school. Heather writes:

> My students love the freedom that they get. They get the opportunity to have choice and that is something that they are embracing. They are very well behaved, respectful to one another, and I haven't had any behavioral issues because they are always doing things and learning in an engaging manner. My students definitely trust me to guide them in their reading choices. I have showed them that I respect them and value their opinion so they have learned to put their trust in me. We just took a trip to the school library (the library is the same size as a classroom with approximately five rows of books. The librarian makes great choices so even though we have limited options, the books that are available to them are great books) and I had many students come up to me and want me to recommend a book for them. That is a great feeling when a student reads a book that you recommended to them based on their interests and things and they end up loving it.

Jeanine and Heather's ideas are not revolutionary; they are simple. By placing the subject at the center of the curriculum and trusting themselves as teachers to engage the students, they can trust their students to respond.

If schools rely on scripted curricula, even in less-extreme cases than the tape recorder scenario above, they run the risk of breaking up the teacher–student–content relationship by giving in to an external *fourth voice*—the outcome—which is developed and assessed externally. Teachers cannot build trust if the curriculum is not involved in the relationship between teacher and student. Like the students in Jeanine's placement, many students do not see a purpose in reading outside of testing. They have been consistently prepared for the tests, but not given the tools to become critical and engaged readers. Montessori (1948/1992) writes of adolescence as "The 'sensitive period' when there should develop the most noble characteristics that would prepare a man to be social, that is to say, a sense of justice and a sense of personal dignity" (p. 63). We believe English teachers can set their primary curricular focuses on the development of such citizens *and* teach the standards.

Rebuilding Trust in Students

One former 10th-grade student in an urban and low-income school, Elise, wrote of her connection to Claudia, the narrator of Toni Morrison's (1970/2000) *The Bluest Eye* and how it had furthered her understanding of the magazine *Seventeen:*

> When I read *Seventeen*, it never addressed real problems I have or the real problem is addressed but the solution always has to do with money I do not have. Why is it expected of girls just to buy a magazine and 'fit in' with everyone else? In *The Bluest Eye* Claudia talks about how she was supposed to want dolls and love Shirley Temple, but she didn't yet. Instead, she speaks of how she wants Bo Jangles to love her if he loves Shirley because she is just as beautiful. I don't think she's old enough to believe yet that her beauty is insufficient, but I think she knows she'll be 'turning' soon. I think this happens to every girl.

Within the context of personal writing, Elise shows a clear understanding here of a Common Core State Standards Initiative for College Reading and Readiness (2010): "Analyze how two or more texts address similar themes or topics in order to build knowledge or to compare the approaches the authors take" (p. 35). This demonstration, however, was not the curriculum objective. Instead, the classroom curriculum offered students a variety of opportunities to compare their own senses of (in)justice with characters in literature.

In a subject-centered literature curriculum, students have the opportunities to grapple with the truths literature offers, like Elise does above; they also (consciously or unconsciously) explore the standards. Explicitly teaching the standards, however, is not the focus of such curriculum (or this book). The focus is on the high school reader, the assets he or she brings to the classroom, and how teachers can shape high schoolers' reading experiences to build on these assets. This requires both veteran and new teachers, like Jeanine, to trust themselves and their students enough to take a few risks. We argue that mastery of the standards happens, explicitly or implicitly, when we trust students as literate beings to explore the full richness of literature.

WHO NEEDS A TRUST-BASED READING CURRICULUM?

This focus on trust is not a frivolous nicety afforded by the genteel assumptions of middle-class White America. Recent studies (Gregory & Ripski, 2008; Rhodes, Stevens, & Hemmings, 2011) have shown that increased trust between students and teachers results in fewer disciplinary referrals and suspensions, which in turn have a direct impact on student success in school and after. Just as jarring as the gap between African Americans, Latinos, Whites, and Asians on the ACT College Readiness Report is the even more strident racial discrepancy between rates of discipline referrals, suspensions, and dropouts (ACT, 2009; Gregory & Ripski, 2008). Educational systems at large also thrive when trust is present, as is detailed by the work of Anthony Bryk and Barbara Schneider (2002).

As high school teachers, we always trusted that all of our students could read. We did not begin each year with a series of engagement activities or hand out graphic organizers each time we read a novel. Instead, we followed the readers. We offered ourselves up as readers and we invited students to read with us.

We have taught a variety of students—from classic AP students, who come from families full of college graduates, to first-generation college hopefuls, to those who will choose professions that do not require college degrees. Throughout this book, you will see their work, words, and interactions with our curriculum. They represent the range of life experiences, cultures, linguistic, and socioeconomic backgrounds often found in cities, and they read for a variety of purposes. As adults, these students continue to remind us of their lasting relationships with literature. They use reading for a range of purposes in their lives, from studying in law school, to traveling across the country, to dealing with the death of a sibling or parent. Of course, they also learned the language of high-stakes tests and how to show on paper that they can read well.

This information is contrary to the message district officials concerned with NCLB rankings often tell teachers: They cannot trust that students can read. So, instead of questioning the test, they are told to question students' abilities. Students are compartmentalized by their abilities or inabilities to choose the correct answer, even when teachers know that such activities fail to help anyone forge a lifelong (or any) relationship with reading. What would happen if teachers and schools defied this deficit assumption, and instead began with the possibility that what all students bring to classrooms and reading experiences will change the way teachers read or teach a novel forever?

OVERVIEW OF A TRUST-BASED READING CURRICULUM

We offer a high school reading curriculum that answers the above question. It brings teachers and students back into the center of the classroom by focusing on their relationships with literature and each other. Such a curriculum does not have to land at one end of the teaching spectrum or the other. Instead, what we have been doing all of these years is teaching all of it—from the whole-class novel, to thematic book groups, to independent reading—and we have been successful. Nel Noddings (1992) believes that education aimed at an "ethic of caring has four major components: modeling, dialogue, practice, and confirmation" (p. 22). We agree and explicitly offer these opportunities in each piece of our curriculum:

- We use whole-class novels to model our reading practices during whole-class novel study and dialogue with students about their own. We also demonstrate to students through the communal reading experience how to build trust, even when the novel has been assigned.
- We use thematic book groups to practice with diverse texts and employ various methods during thematic book groups to engage, observe, and support students in their reading (student-led seminars, small reading communities, journals, etc.). We also demonstrate to students through a low-risk, small-group environment how to explore reading independence and build trusting relationships.
- We use independent reading to share the responsibility and power of book selection with our students and to confirm who students are as readers. By providing students with choice, we confirm and valorize their identities as readers and further build trust.

All of these pieces include, at their core, an unwavering commitment to dialogue with the readers in our classrooms. Because the experience of reading is open-ended, we cannot prescribe our methods as answers to classroom problems. Instead, we propose an overhaul to typical classroom reading curricula by systematically moving between self- and group-selected books and teacher-selected texts for the whole class. We propose the I (teacher) Choose, You (student) Choose curriculum, which allows for both student choice and teacher expertise. This increases students' engagement with the books they choose, but it also increases their willingness to work with teachers and trust their book choices.

USING THIS BOOK

In the chapters that follow, we use a series of reflective invitations to help teacher readers rediscover trust in themselves and in their students. We begin in Chapter 1 by guiding you back to your love of reading; from there, we help you in Chapter 2 to develop a philosophy for teaching high school reading. We ground the remainder of the book in this personal philosophy and proceed to show you how you can implement this into your classrooms by using the I Choose, You Choose curriculum described in Chapter 3. Our methods chapters begin with a whole-class text (Chapter 4), move into book groups (Chapter 5), and end with the independent reading cycle (Chapter 6). As you work through each methods chapter, you will begin to create your own I Choose, You Choose curriculum for your specific context through the "Extend your Thinking" sections. Our classroom examples, which range from urban to rural and suburban contexts, should help you interweave trust-building methods (small reading communities, critically engaging lessons, student-led seminars, artistic response, drama, and dialogue) into an I Choose, You Choose curriculum that honors your own teaching of reading philosophy.

We hope you will use this book in whatever capacity fits your needs. Our proposal has three overarching intentions: to reintroduce trust into the classroom, reclaim the decency that was lost when NCLB began to require us to ferret out the inadequacies of each child, and rediscover the English classroom as a place of possibility and power.

CHAPTER 1

Trusting Our Ways as Readers

Photo by Michael Smyth

WE BEGIN THIS CHAPTER by listing some of the concerns many high school English teachers have when trying to engage in meaningful reading experiences with their students:

1. Students need to learn to read for specific academic purposes.
2. Students should read only certain books to make them better readers.
3. Students need to answer test questions correctly.
4. Students need to prepare themselves as readers for a narrow goal: college.
5. Students need to be able to read, understand, and follow test directions (however complicated).
6. Students need to demonstrate, via a predetermined increase in test scores, that they are reading better than they were last year.

7. Students need to be able to identify certain aspects of a passage or poem and answer questions about its literary qualities.

The list could go on. What might you add? Because of the external pressures for outcomes-based teaching, teachers often find themselves engulfed in doubt about their own capacities to teach. This focus on outcomes serves to erode self-reliance as educators and causes teachers to doubt students' abilities. In reality, the demanded outcomes are not serving the intellectual minds in our classrooms.

Miriam Raider-Roth (2005) writes that while our loudest educational voices declare that testing children will build a foundation of strong knowledge, it is actually "resilient, trustworthy relationships in school [that] are the bedrock of learning" (p. 19). She argues that when children have this type of schooling experience, they learn to trust their knowledge, and, as a result, are more willing to take risks with it, grow and change, and form "relationships that will sustain them as adults" (p. 18). She proposes four central factors in a trusting teaching-learning relationship: "1. the teacher's capacity to be connected to the student, 2. the teacher's genuine interest in nurturing the students' own ideas, 3. collaborative study on the part of the teacher and the student 4. an environment in which trust can prevail" (p. 30). These four criteria require teachers to trust themselves as readers while simultaneously infusing that trust into their classroom practices.

Raider-Roth's work examines practices we have road tested in our classrooms for years. More important, she emphasizes what many great teachers already know: Trust is an essential component in classrooms where lifelong learning, literacy, and interconnectedness thrive. The examples in the following sections illustrate how teachers can use connectedness, reverence, collaboration, and a safe environment to build trust with their students.

CONNECTEDNESS

Human beings are social animals. Some are introverts, some extroverts, and some are a little of both. Regardless, positive relationships can have an important role in our lives. High school students are in a time of experimentation, much of which is social. Teachers can provide them with opportunities to develop connectedness by experimenting with positive social relationships, especially with students who are different from themselves. Because it is ripe with universal themes, social issues and dilemmas, and opportunities for inference and analysis, literature is an incredible way for students to see social relationships unfold on the page. They can also build and compare their opinions to others in the class. Literature welcomes the creative mind. Joe, a former student of ours, states:

> In my English class I felt like the books gave me a chance to get
> to know people I might not normally talk to. The way we shared
> things was important too. Like, if I believed something because of
> my background or whatever, I wasn't afraid to bring it up in a book
> discussion, even though I knew other people might not agree. There
> was just something about it. I always felt like I was okay to share
> my thoughts and a lot of times my ideas changed because of the
> discussion I might have with someone who disagreed.

Joe's opinions about the world evolved through his communal study of literature. For some students, this process happens easily, but it is important to consider ways to scaffold connectedness for all students in a literature classroom.

Building a Connected Classroom

Although he had done well on all the high-stakes tests and gotten good grades, Chris admits he had never read a full-length novel—or learned to love reading—until the 10th grade. In this particular class, his reading experience was memorable because the teacher created a trusting environment for students.

Chris's teacher, Anne, had a system in place that allowed her to build trust with students throughout the year. Without her assistance, students knew how to find their portfolios, reading logs, and extra classroom supplies. They also knew how to use the computers, classroom library, and storage cabinets. The classroom was constantly abuzz with working students, but this was no accident. Anne spent time teaching her students how to independently use the space in a safe and respectful way. She reminded them frequently, without fussing, when they veered off course.

She also took simple actions by greeting students at the door at the start and end of every class. She held community meetings and encouraged dialogue through introductory journals to focus them. The community meetings allowed students to briefly come together as a class and share news by passing an object such as a rock. Anne invited each student to share what he or she was feeling with the circle, or pass. This allowed her to quietly take the pulse of the class, and offered students time to come together as colleagues in a nonthreatening sharing session. Because it was brief and had parameters (everyone had 15 seconds to share and pass the object), it made instructional time easier because Anne understood the status of the class before delving into the lesson. Equally integral to Anne's approach was that she spent less time talking and more time listening and coaching. She designed lessons that were full of practice opportunities, so she could watch students in action. She not only trusted herself to be connected to them, but she made it possible and transparent by setting up the classroom environment and workday with that objective in mind.

Robert Marzano (2006) proposed a new taxonomy of educational objectives that builds on Bloom's taxonomy (1956), adding *metacognitive* and *self-system* levels. The metacognitive system organizes how we think, including setting goals and processes. The self-system is where decisions are made about whether or not we will try a new task. These two new levels work interdependently to engage students in their tasks. To engage students' self-systems, Anne used her classroom observations to design mini-lessons that provided students with focused literary tasks aimed at increasing reading capabilities and elevating student confidence in reading. To engage students' metacognitive selves, she used introductory journals, community meetings, and guided practice sessions to heighten students' awareness of why and how reading might benefit them.

In Chris's class, each day had a similar pattern: Students quietly found their seats, copied the homework assignment and reviewed the daily agenda, and completed the initial exercise to calm their minds and focus on the class ahead. This exercise was directly connected to the guiding questions (discussed in Chapter 3) that Anne used to make her curriculum both personally relevant and thematically connected throughout the year.

Anne's methods exude confidence in her ability to share control with her students. To set this up, however, she had to first trust in her ability to do so. A teacher should first prepare a workspace for students and set parameters for interaction within that workspace. Opportunities to listen, observe, and engage students in Marzano's (2006) new taxonomy are often absent when students do not know how to work within the boundaries of the classroom. Equally important, the students' capacity for risk-taking diminishes when they are unsure of the classroom patterns and expectations. So, establishing a daily ritual can help students and teachers learn how to operate in a trusting space. Figure 1.1 depicts a typical 55-minute schedule and the components within that time frame that can lead to connectedness.

Getting Started

Before you begin planning a reading curriculum for high school students, we ask that you consider two questions and make them the focus

Figure 1.1. Typical Schedule for Creating a Connected Classroom

Time	Student Tasks	Level of Engagement with Marzano's New Taxonomy (2006)
3–5 minutes	Students arrive; teacher greets everyone at the door. Students find their seats, copy homework, and review the agenda. Students begin journal prompt.	Metacognitive Self
5–10 minutes	Students meet in a circle and pass an object to share one sentence from their journals, a brief idea about the prompt, or anything that might be weighing on them. Teacher takes notes for future lessons.	Metacognitive self
10–15 minutes	Students return to classroom space for mini-lesson	Self-system
20–25 minutes	Students work in groups, pairs, or independently on an experience tied to the mini-lesson (this could be guided practice with teacher coaching, small group project, performances, or reading, seminar, etc.). Teacher rotates, coaches, observes, listens, and takes notes.	Metacognitive and self-systems
2–5 minutes	Closure	

of your daily classroom maintenance to help increase your classroom's capacity for connectedness:

1. What would my connected classroom look like (separate seminar areas, reading libraries, arrangement of desks, placement of supplies)?
2. How can I establish routines and procedures that foster a safe and respectful space and give students opportunities to be connected to me, the material, and one another instead of opportunities to become disconnected by misbehaving, misusing the materials, or disrespecting the space and people in it? What do these routines and procedures look like?

Keep your answers simple. Classroom communities need not be bombarded by extensive and complicated lists of rules, procedures, and routines.

Students and teachers have trouble maintaining such elaborate systems. As you plan, make sure that your goals are clear, uncomplicated, and achievable on a daily basis. Be prepared to revisit these goals if the classroom climate begins to deteriorate. Remember, if we wish to be connected to our students, we must do the hard work necessary to take care of these forming relationships. We cannot fulfill a capacity for connectedness in an environment that works against it, where we must spend all of our energy and focus on the pieces that are broken. If we want houses that are clean, organized, and welcoming, we have to do the work to set up and to maintain these systems. It is the same in our classrooms.

REVERENCE

In order to effectively listen, observe, and use that data to structure the experiences of a classroom, teachers have to honestly, respectfully, and genuinely be interested in what students offer the classrooms. Without this reverence, trust cannot be built, regardless of the routines they establish, the choices they allow, or the number of high interest books they let students read. Paulo Freire (1992/2002) writes: "The educational practice of a progressive option will never be anything but an adventure in unveiling. It will always be an experiment in bringing out the truth" (p. 1). To do this, a teacher has to trust that she can find out what her students know through dialogue about a subject and uncover "ways for them to go *beyond* their state of thinking" (Horton, Bell, Gaventa, & Peters, 1990, p. 98). This requires an interest in both student and subject, but, more important, a passion for the process of knowing more.

We can return to Chris's story with this idea of reverence in mind: One of his primary reasons for wanting suddenly to read in the 10th grade was that he began to see the experience of reading differently. Through his relationship with his teacher and the other students in the class, he began to dialogue about books, learn to choose reading for his own purposes, and search for personal meaning in texts. Suddenly, he existed in a classroom community that cared deeply about what he brought to a text and took away; it was a classroom concerned with the process of "unveiling" (Freire, 1992/2002, p. 1). In this process, reading became important for his own experience, not just for the experience of schooling.

This change in Chris speaks to the developmental shift in adolescence toward building judgment, risk-taking, and social involvement, at which time he also discovered reading as a way to inform his experience more richly. Dayan, Bernard, Olliac, Mailhes, and Kermarrec (2010) write:

Both the quality of their emotional experiences (valence and intensity) and the judgments of their peers contribute to the fine-tuning of adolescents' actions and values. This process of self-definition through action ultimately makes an important contribution to the relatively stable self-representations of adulthood. . . . Risk-taking contributes to the efficient shaping of the most highly evolved parts of the brain that are responsible for the "sapience" which characterizes the human species. (pp. 280, 284)

If we consider students similar to Chris the median, what about those students who are at either end of the spectrum—the students who, in doing poorly on the standardized tests, are confronted with more test prep or the students who, in doing well on tests, are not challenged? Not only are all of these students being denied opportunities to see literature as a way to question or validate their own experiences, but their reading lives are void of experiences that can enhance their social and cognitive development, thus furthering their intellectual capacities as adults. The classroom spaces they occupy as readers are void of reverence for the individual mind.

Building Reverence for Subject and Students

To find out what our students know and then construct environments ripe for knowing more, teachers have to first understand what they know and why they know it. Teachers cannot establish this place of respect and honesty with readers without first finding it in themselves. A teacher who has a deep and complex understanding of her interior will be more successful in implementing this on the exterior (her classroom). So, we invite you to complete the following activity, inspired by Alfred Tatum's (2009) *textual lineage* exercise:

1. On a piece of paper, draw a line down the center. Make five to seven ticks (equally spaced) on the line. These ticks represent critical years in your own life.
2. Take a few moments to journal about these years.
3. Reflect on the timeline. For each of these critical years, think of a book you read that may have provided insight along the way.

We would venture to say that by the time a future English teacher enters college, she has a good understanding about the importance of reading in her life. Most English teachers choose the field because they love the subject. Literature and writing have helped them form identities. When teachers place this love of subject at the center of their classrooms, the possibilities are endless. Students can be energized by a subject-focused classroom.

Getting Started

The first step in this process begins with teachers remembering their love of subject. Use your reading timeline to answer the following questions:

1. Why do you love to read?
2. Does it energize you to share great titles with friends and colleagues? Why?
3. What have books taught you?

In the process of remembering your love of subject, you might also remember your competence in the subject area. English teachers know a lot about reading and writing.

English teachers should allow students to cultivate connections to literature, not because it will help them on tests, but because the benefits of lifelong reading are powerful and purposeful. Literature changed our lives and we want our students to be open to this possibility. With that assumption in mind, we propose a variety of methods in the following chapters that draw students closer to the subject. Nevertheless, these methods must have at their foundation a classroom environment that is intentionally prepared so that students can explore the subject fully. These are spaces which are ripe for knowing more.

COLLABORATIVE INQUIRY

Excellent literature teachers constantly add to both their personal and professional reading lists and frequently share titles with others. The problem arises when teachers confront the amount of material to be covered in the timeline provided. It is truly a daunting balancing act. Palmer (2007) writes, "This sense of responsibility cannot be faulted. But the conclusion that we draw from it—that we must sacrifice space in order to cover the field—is based on the false premise that *space* and *stuff* are mutually exclusive" (p. 123). Instead, we agree that when teachers open the space of the classroom for mutual inquiry with students, the "stuff" gets covered, but in a way that allows students to see themselves as trusted co-investigators who can make choices about reading, structure responses, and discover what the subject can offer them on their own journeys. When we as teachers don't trust the power of our subjects or our connections as English teachers to them, we cannot lead this inquiry effectively. Tasks aimed at producing assessable results fill classrooms and, sadly, provide no information about students' connections to literature.

The author's purpose for any text is not for readers to complete a study guide for each chapter or take a test when they finish reading. Consider this quotation from Frederick Douglass (1845/2008):

> I have found that, to make a contented slave, it . . . is necessary to make a thoughtless one. It is necessary to darken his moral and mental vision, and, as far as possible, to annihilate the power of reason. He must be able to detect no inconsistencies in slavery; he must be made to feel that slavery is right; and he can be brought to that only when he ceases to be a man. (p. 99)

If teachers look at the quotation from the perspective of how much content they must cover with the text, they might get embroiled in an agenda that makes the historical period of slavery the focus. This is certainly the most detached and, frankly, easy approach for study. If students look at this as an isolated period in our history, they can have the opportunity to explore it without guilt, fear, or any investigation of the permeating impact slavery has on our society; thus, it has little relevance to students' lives today beyond needing to know about it for school. This is an incredible tragedy.

As passionate readers in their subject areas, however, teachers know the above passage offers more to students. The process of placing the text at the center can begin by asking guiding questions. Guiding questions are the open-ended, unanswerable questions that guide readings. In our classrooms, they stemmed from themes and issues we discovered our students discussing in relation to the work they did in our classes. We discuss these types of questions more thoroughly in Chapters 3 and 4. For our purposes here, however, the guiding questions we might choose could be: What is slavery? How do we become enslaved? Are we currently enslaved? Why or why not? What does it mean, according to Douglass, to be a man? Through monologue projects, dramatic role play, dialogue with teachers and peers, and personal writing such as journal responses, students can explore (not simply answer) these questions as they pertain to the here and now of their lives. It is one thing to say that slavery began and ended in a certain time of history, but it is another entirely to explore Douglass's message about the human psyche, slavery, and those implications for today's times.

Building Collaborative Inquiry with Mandated Reading Lists

When teachers look at the Douglass piece together with students, they can see why it is a classic. His words can apply to so many current situations in all of our lives. Megan, a White middle-class university student, first encountered this text and its guiding questions as a part of her graduate English methods class. She wrote, "I never knew that a book which seems to be about a subject so far rwmoved from me could teach me so much about education, access to education, and the freedom it offers all of us. After reading this book and talking with my small reading group, I find myself questioning my language and assumptions about difference." She went on to discuss how the classroom activities she participated in helped her make these connections: "When I first started reading this, I was overwhelmed, but when we did the scavenger hunt, paired it with McGruder's (2003) *A Right to be Hostile,* and did the letter-writing activity between Douglass and Huey, I started to see its importance for me as a White woman and teacher." A critical co-investigation of this text provides students with opportunities to trust their own experiences and compare them to Douglass's insights.

Students in our high school classrooms have explored Douglass's work through multigenre pieces on their own lives, investigations into media and its targets, global inquiries, and social action projects. They demonstrated to us what they know about Douglass's words and, in response, we asked them more questions and pointed them toward paths of greater knowledge.

Getting Started

For English teachers, the bulk of the content comes in exploring reading and writing with students. In looking at the typical high school reading curriculum, we realize that there are often certain required texts. For many reasons, these lists are problematic. Nevertheless, for our purposes here, we need to embrace the lists and discuss how these pieces can operate as staples in a thriving high school English classroom. They can build on established foundations of trust and open the roads of co-investigation.

If you have a mandated reading list of whole-class novels, jot them down, including title and author(s). Although these titles may be initially difficult for students, there are multiple reasons (good and bad) why they are considered timeless. (We will discuss the power of the whole-class novel in more detail in Chapter 4.) To help you embrace the lists and discuss how these pieces can operate as staples in a thriving high school English classroom, we would like to focus on the good reasons. After making your list of novels, write down the timeless main ideas from each novel and how to use them as building blocks for trust. Figure 1.2 provides a sample we created using four mandated titles from our district for 9th and 10th grade.

Figure 1.2. Main Ideas and Building Blocks for Trust in Mandated Reading

Title	Timeless Main Ideas	Building Blocks for Trust
The Great Gatsby by F. Scott Fitzgerald (1925/2004)	Love, power, money, betrayal, isolation, renewal.	Each of these main ideas can serve as the building blocks for expanding on issues our students see every day involving money, desire, and power, and the implications of these messages in their lives.
Romeo and Juliet by William Shakespeare (1597/1992)	Love, power, money, betrayal, family pressures, youth, violence, suicide.	The play provides so many avenues for critical inquiry and the implications of adult judgments concerning adolescent love. The language itself shows students how language changes over time and the playfulness of English syntax and vocabulary.
Narrative of the Life of Frederick Douglass by Frederick Douglass (1845/2008)	Education, freedom, friendship, hatred, betrayal, violence, self-discovery.	The ways in which we self-educate or are forced to educate ourselves outside of what the schoolhouse offers can be explored. Classical rhetoric and persuasion pervade the text, opening it to rigorous analysis of form. It inspires students to write powerfully about subjects that matter deeply to them.
Night by Elie Wiesel (1960/1982)	Violence, faith, hope, hatred, betrayal, adversity, strength, family.	This is an opportunity for students to explore faith, hope, resilience, and strength. Wiesel gives us a glimpse into his own experiences and the tests of all these in his lifetime. It is not difficult for students to see how all of these pieces can be tested so often in their worlds.

CO-INVESTIGATION AND SAFE CLASSROOM ENVIRONMENTS

Literature calls upon readers to be vulnerable. If students are to explore Douglass's messages and the implications in their own lives, they risk opening themselves up to discussing their fears and faults. If teachers see themselves as co-investigators on this journey, they risk the same fate.

For many, this is a difficult task; new teachers might see this as relinquishing power, and veteran teachers might balk at such a paradigm shift in their classrooms. The reality is that every single day, students co-produce the learning in classrooms. Engaging them in inquiry yields stronger learning and models thoughtful, resilient, creative habits of mind that are so essential for 21st-century learning. Teachers often learn that they need to be in power. From that claim of power comes a sense of classroom control.

John Dewey (1916) writes of schools: "The environment consists of those conditions that promote or hinder, stimulate or inhibit, the *characteristic* activities of a living being" (p. 13). He explains that the school can serve as a special environment for young people in that it can re-create qualities of our lived environments within the school, but in ways that provide students with a simplified set of characteristics of our society.

With the Frederick Douglass reading, we did an ongoing "scavenger hunt" with students. This is a simple way to scaffold the co-investigation of Douglass's themes. For example, if we look at the above quotation, Douglass writes: "It is necessary to darken his moral and mental vision, and, as far as possible, to annihilate the power of reason." Instead of asking students a series of teacher- or textbook-generated questions about this quotation, we invite them instead to *live with it*. They jot the quotation down on a small slip of paper and place it in their pockets or a safe space for keeping. We put it in our own pockets as well. We ask them to read it several times during the course of the day (on the bus, at home, at school) and just think about it. In class the next day, we asked what they came up with and shared our experiences too. Many of them were anxious to tell us how Douglass's words influenced their perceptions. They saw this quotation in action through television, music, radio advertisements, billboards, and on the Internet. We did this throughout the book, ultimately asking students to select their own lines to carry with them. In the end, many claimed the book drove them crazy, and they couldn't find as much joy in reading a magazine or listening to a certain song because Douglass made them think about these pieces in their lives differently.

In activities similar to this one, teachers can use Douglass to do the work of bringing students back to literature. The activity fuses Douglass's words from a wholly different experience, and gives students opportunities to apply them to their own lives, without judgment. It shows students (and teachers who participate alongside students) why literature can be timeless and how connected we are in the human experience. Through this presentation, we can safeguard the explorations of adolescents and, through direction in the subject area, we stimulate growth. It is within this type of classroom that dialogue happens.

On the surface, this might not offer the control teachers believe they are supposed to maintain in their classrooms. There is no test to see if students really "got" the lines in the scavenger hunt. In fact, some of them didn't initially do the activity. There is, however, a difference between a highly *ordered* environment where students can safely experiment with the choices Dewey describes and a highly *controlled* environment (with a clear hierarchy of power to influence this control), where students have few choices, and operate in fear. In this situation, we relied on the influence of the group to inspire the more reluctant students. When those who didn't explore the quotation initially heard the conversation in class the next day, they were sure to think about their quotations for the next class. Instead of punishing those students, we offered them a chance to step back and try again. We found that it only took one false start to join the group.

GETTING STARTED ON BUILDING A SAFE ENVIRONMENT FOR ALL STUDENTS

In thinking about the environment you re-create in your classroom, consider these questions with a mandated text you chose from your list:

1. How can I find out what my students know about the subjects of this text?
2. How can I clarify these subjects so that they are easier for my students to explore in our classroom?
3. What personal guidance do I hope they will get from this text?
4. How can I prepare the environment (activities, projects, journals, seminars, etc.) so that students can gain this guidance and expand upon it for their own purposes?

In the second part of this exercise we ask you to predict your own behavior through further self-reflection; this step is important because it safeguards teachers from entering into conversations that cause discomfort. We remind you that it is okay to work within your comfort zone initially and gradually work toward taking more risks with students.

1. What answers/experiences am I comfortable hearing from my students?
2. What answers/experiences am I uncomfortable hearing?
3. Am I comfortable making choices about what to simplify or include in our study of this text? What makes me comfortable or uncomfortable?
4. Do I trust myself to guide my students into some unknown explorations of this text? What could be the benefits of exploring the unknown with them?

5. Can I create valuable learning experiences for them that continually build on what they already know about this text? How can I monitor this as we work?

When we collaborate with our students, we have to understand the profundity of the sharing experience. Often, what makes us uncomfortable also makes us wiser. For example, in the activity above, it is difficult not to address the blatant fact that it was done in a mixed racial and socioeconomic classroom with White teachers. It might be quite easy to discuss slavery in a historical context, but it is something entirely different to apply Douglass's words to the here and now, especially if that teacher brings in her own reflections on the quotation.

In one such instance, Brian, one of our African American male students, commented that he thought about the quotation when he heard a group of White male students (who were also in the class) listening to a classic Public Enemy song and singing all the words. He noted that the words sounded strange to him coming from a White person's mouth. He then added that he didn't think the music was meant for White people. One of the White students he cited asked him what he was listening to lately. He responded with an album title from the more mainstream rapper Jay-Z. This inspired an entire class conversation about race, music, slavery, and Frederick Douglass, in which students referred frequently back to how the mainstream media can "annihilate the power of reason" for them. We invited our students to explore their worlds in the context of Douglass and they did. More important, they did so in a way we could not have predicted or been completely comfortable and knowledgeable to guide them. Instead, during that session, we had to mediate, listen, and learn. In the wrong environment, however, what makes us uncomfortable can also isolate us.

As you make choices and prepare environments for students, keep in mind that a safe environment is not always a comfortable environment; instead, a safe environment can be one where students and teacher trust their discomforts, are free to discuss and explore them, and build on their new knowledge of subject, but are supported in this process. In the context above, all of these were in place. As a result, a conversation that could have been contentious was actually a critical, yet respectful, dialogue.

FINAL THOUGHTS

Building trusting classrooms necessitates hard work. Such places require constant and impeccable maintenance, the cultivation of healthy relationships, and a desire to sort out obstacles through meaningful discussions. It would be easier and cleaner to follow a study guide or teach students how to correctly answer comprehension questions on a reading test. In those practices, the teacher can be eternally comfortable and the students forever detached from the deeper lessons in an excellent text. Students will pass, teachers will get paid, but neither will be the wiser. We believe in the reading classrooms where the hard work happens.

Extend Your Thinking

Reflecting on what you've learned in this chapter, write what you believe your students should gain from the reading curriculum in your classroom. Consider your goal statement and compare it with the obstacles you face as a teacher. Is it worth it to pursue your goal? Why or why not?

Now, rewrite your statement and list three steps you could take every day in your classroom to make that statement possible. This is your teaching of reading philosophy. You will revisit this statement several times throughout the book.

CHAPTER 2

Trust Me
Learning to Build Trust in Students

Photo by Michael Smyth

I F YOU HAVE EVER met an adolescent who claims to hate reading for school, ask her what goes on in English class. It will not take you long to discover the source of her problem. She might tell you the English teacher is nice or smart, but we would venture to guess that student would also tell you that she does not trust the teacher to help guide her personal or academic reading activities.

Adolescents are at a time in their lives when their egocentrism evolves to include their perceptions of others, which often center on how others feel about them (Elkind, 1967). As a result, adolescents are often keenly aware of the nuances in classrooms and relationships. They can be critical of each other and their teachers because of their own perceptions of self in relation to others and vice versa. A high school reading curriculum should have personal relevance and encourage autonomy, but it will not work unless adolescents can work independently and interdependently in a nurturing environment. Because reading can be so personal in these classrooms, teachers need great care in establishing spaces that meet the needs of the new egocentrism teenagers experience. These pieces cannot be developed with scripted curricula, where the trust placed in students and teacher perceptions of their trust become compromised in an effort to cover material.

When George Hillocks Jr. (2009) writes that "all, or nearly all, students are capable of learning what our strongest students learn" he calls on us to trust in their capabilities (p. 24). There are, however, tremendous obstacles. Deficit models permeate our educational system. The result of this, as Rathunde and Csikszentmihalyi (2005) remind us, is that there is a "narrowing of perspective that increasingly equates intellectual skills with a thin set of cognitive skills that ignore affect and take the 'body' out of the mind" (p. 75). They write that teachers in such schools, because of the pressures of high-stakes testing, are much less likely to trust or tap into the intrinsic motivation of students to learn. What is even more disparaging is the potential for such practices to remove the "'body' [from] the mind" (p. 75). In a high school English classroom, it is impossible to foster a lifelong love of literature through dialogue by only teaching skills. When we remove the human element from schooling, we risk alienating teenagers when they desperately need trusting relationships to strengthen connections between their actions (body) with thoughts (mind).

TRUSTING PRACTICES THAT RECOGNIZE STUDENTS' ASSETS

So, how do teachers find their ways back to students? Many find this to be a complicated endeavor. Consider student teacher Janie. Janie was excited about her first observation in an urban and low-income school. She learned the reading workshop method in her English Education courses, practiced implementing it with her fellow classmates on the college level, developed an intense familiarity with Young Adult Literature, and professed excitement about spending time with young people. On the first day of her placement, however, she found a 9th-grade classroom filled with students and no teacher. According to the teacher next door, the previous teacher had not returned after break. Janie reported to her professors that workshop or engagement activities with her students would be impossible because of their behavior and lack of skills. She noted that students could not sit still, they disrespected one another verbally, talked throughout class, and several struggled to read one page of grade-level text or said they hated reading and would not even try.

Janie's description of the class, like many initial descriptions of classrooms where parameters are suddenly nonexistent, focuses on the students. She used words like "wild" and "out of control" to describe students. All of Janie's training and excitement did not stop her from using this kind of language in relation to students or from overlooking their assets as readers. We believe the reasoning for this is threefold:

1. Top-down models of schooling surround new and experienced teachers. Here, they learn to impart it, not respectfully discover it as a community of learners.
2. It is easier to blame the students, their backgrounds, and responses to a failing system than it is to reexamine the structural elements that guide human behavior. When test scores corroborate student inadequacies, the situation becomes more complicated.
3. Instead of working within environments that problem solve and collaborate on behalf of students, many teachers are still surrounded by peers who quickly dismiss the capabilities of students and instead label them as "unteachable."

It is important to name the ideologies that keep teachers entrenched in language that refers to students as animals and erodes even fleeting notions of trust in schools. In this situation, Janie emerged from the classroom and found a group of colleagues in the school who agreed with her initial assumptions about the students. As a result, they made no concrete plan to support Janie or the students in the classroom.

Clearly, Janie's situation is dismal. There are many schools where teachers collaborate and work with students in a different capacity. Teachers can counteract some of the aforementioned issues by providing students with varied literate experiences in a workshop classroom. Cathy Roller (1996) writes: "Rather than view children as capable or disabled, workshop classrooms assume that children are different, that each child is unique and has special interests and abilities, and that differences are normal" (p. 7).

Workshop classrooms honor the learners within. They assume that students have valid interests, can and will choose books to read for pleasure, need to have conversations with teachers and peers about these books, and will choose to write about their responses through journal entries and letters. These experiences offer teachers opportunities to observe students at work and better plan instruction within the literature curriculum. Equally, teachers can model positive ways human beings can interact: through genuine listening and careful interactions with one another. This type of modeling allows students in this developmental phase to more clearly interpret others' actions and words in relation to themselves.

USING TRUSTING PRACTICES WITH INDEPENDENT, COMPETITIVE, AND SOCIAL LEARNERS

In our workshop model (the I Choose, You Choose curriculum), we offer a variety of settings in which teachers can observe students, coach, and adapt instruction. We believe this works for high school classrooms because it offers students multiple opportunities for interaction in a classroom—tapping into their independent, social, and competitive learning styles, and safely pushing them toward new learning risks. It works for high school teachers because it allows them to witness student interactions in multiple learning experiences and use these observations to strengthen, alter, and extend the curriculum for specific learners.

Consider these three types of learners: the independent learner (head down, buried in work), the competitive learner (head up, pencil moving, mind closed), and the social learner (mouth moving, body turned to others). Each of these learners can benefit from trusting reading workshop environments; with the right set of variables, however, each can quickly contribute to spaces where trust vanishes.

Independence

Elizabeth is an independent learner. She does not bend easily to the influence of her peers or teacher. Instead, she comes to school with a set of skills and type of confidence that reflect her life in a single-parent household and now as a new mother. She is not afraid to pick up a new text, read it, and write about it for class. However, she has little time to read for pleasure outside of school.

Some days, she is distant and withdrawn from the reading workshop, but on other occasions she is quick to offer opinions and judgments about a variety of topics. Although she cares about her grades, they tend to fall and rise throughout the year. She struggles with whole-class texts because they don't always pique her interest, and she resists books offered by teachers she doesn't feel comfortable being with.

A workshop environment offers learners like Elizabeth *time to read*, which is often the single most quantifiable barrier to independent reading. Providing adolescents with time to read in a quiet and orderly classroom setting shows them that we acknowledge and respect their busy lives. It also invites them to see reading as a potentially restful activity.

With independent learners, it is important to remember the assets they bring to a classroom. Their senses of independence can be models for other students. Equally important, we can use workshop methods in whole-class text study (as we discuss further in Chapter 4), so that learners like Elizabeth still have time to read in class, make choices about the texts, construct responses that give them autonomy, and learn independently, in small groups, and with the entire class. This kind of whole-class text study might benefit learners like Elizabeth because it also offers an opportunity to experience a text in a way they might not independently choose.

We can further build trust with these students by sharing our own reading, exchanging titles, and dialoguing. This increases the possibility that learners like Elizabeth will trust us to choose and plan a whole-class text study with *their* needs and interests in mind.

Competition

Ethan thrives on his routine Monday question for his teacher: "What is my percentage right now in English?" For him, it is not about the letter grade, but how he is ranking in percentages. His goal is to get a 100% (or higher) in English this quarter. He enjoys predicting what will be on the test, trying to uncover patterns in teacher feedback, and showing his fellow students how they are wrong by using textual examples. Then, after taking the test, he spends the day discussing his answers with friends and gauging his potential errors. Ethan is a role model for the high-stakes testing culture in America. He learns and plays the game of school. For teachers, he might seem like he could adapt to any schooling circumstance as long as he is being graded, praised, or evaluated.

What happens, however, when we ask Ethan what he likes to read? It is highly possible that without scrolling through the list of class novels he has read, he will not be able to tell us honestly what draws him into a book. As a result, Ethan morphs into the most challenging learner for a workshop environment where praise is nonexistent, and students read for the real purpose and joy of finding answers to their own questions about the world. He will continue to ask the teacher pointed questions to extract praise, some sort of assessment, or status in the classroom.

It takes a lot of dialogue with learners like Ethan to get them to trust in classrooms in which focused feedback is in the form of a dialogue, grades are not given for every task, and students are learning collaboration rather than competition. When working with competitive learners like Ethan, a crucial focus is to develop a dialogue of trust that helps them understand clearly the expectations. Because so many of the expectations are contrary to their habits, it takes time for learners similar to Ethan not to resist the workshop approach. These learners need teachers to recognize them daily by talking with them about topics that are not related to school achievement. Short conversations as they enter the classroom help these learners feel personally acknowledged outside of assessment while modeling dialogue with others in a way that reveres both sides.

Socialization

Anthony is a social learner. Similar to Ethan, he thrives on attention, specifically the attention he receives as the high school basketball team's star. On the surface, he appears to snub classroom learning and embraces the learning he can get from his peers through talking and playful banter. Workshop classrooms can be difficult for learners similar to Anthony because, like Ethan, their motivations are often external. They are constantly seeking or holding onto the approval of their peer group by maintaining a certain persona. They might be learners who tell us that reading is boring simply because their friends are not readers. Or, during independent reading time, they might be prone to sleeping or whispering to their classmates who have directed their attention away from them.

Not surprisingly, it often takes a considerable amount of dialogue and work, false starts, and failures on the part of a teacher to help these learners find books that speak to them. Teachers should see working with learners like Anthony as opportunities to invest in students' lives outside of school. Researching students' lives, showing up at their extracurricular activities, or becoming patrons where they work are small gestures that help us see students in different contexts (and vice versa), and give us opportunities to dialogue with them in their safe spaces. These opportunities also bring us closer to helping them find the literature that speaks to them.

Equally important, having learners like Anthony in the classroom offers plentiful opportunities to engage students in small learning communities like the ones we describe in Chapter 5. Such communities allow these learners to maximize their social skills but learn to respect the influence their peer groups have on them. In addition, these communities help social learners learn to trust the environment of the classroom, see their peers as resources, and move into spaces where they might take risks.

MAKING TRUSTING PRACTICES WORK WITH ALL STUDENTS

In the average classroom, we have plenty of students like Elizabeth, Ethan, and Anthony. Unlike the outside world that our classrooms reflect, however, teachers are expected (daily) to control behavior, develop curricula that help students excel on high-stakes tests, implement assessments with quantifiable outcomes, and keep everyone on task. These duties often clash with the real work involved in schooling for a critical consciousness. They comprise what Paulo Freire (1970/1993) describes as the banking concept of education: "In this view, the person is not a conscious being (*corpo consciente*); he or she is rather a possessor of consciousness: an empty 'mind' passively open to the receptions of deposits of reality from the world outside" (p. 75). The premise of our book and curriculum is that teachers can and should strive to be "humanist" educators, who teach conscious beings in a perpetual state of transformation. This type of teacher does not wait for students to wake up to the world. Instead, Freire writes,

> Her efforts must coincide with those of the student to engage in critical thinking and the quest for mutual humanization. Her efforts must be imbued with a profound trust in people and their creative power. To do this, they must be partners with the students in their relations with them. (p. 75)

Although many teachers agree with the above premise, it is often difficult for them to imagine how it would be achieved in a system that demands compliance with prescriptive practices. Teachers fear that if they are to learn alongside students, they are also going to lose control of the class.

We constantly hear teachers and administrators comment that a certain teacher "cannot control her class." Students spill over into the hallways, shoot paper wads around the room, and disrespect one another and the environment. If we use common rhetoric for these types of classrooms, they are "running wild." So, when we visit teachers in the field or talk about trust with them, it is not surprising that many, similar to Janie, tell us that trusting practices are impossible in their schools or classrooms.

We invite you to imagine a high school English classroom where Elizabeth has time to read her chosen parenting books, talk with other students about them, and use them to uncover themes and ideas in whole class novel study—with the community she's found in the classroom. In that community, Ethan stops comparing himself to her and instead starts to compare himself to himself. He reads endlessly, as if in some kind of private competition with himself. Now, he finds it easier to talk about texts he likes, make connections across these texts and with the texts others are reading, and dives fearlessly into the whole-class novel because he trusts the process. Elizabeth and Ethan are in a small reading community with Anthony, where they are reading *Sacred Hoops: Spiritual Lessons of a Hardwood Warrior* (1995) by Phil Jackson and Hugh Delehanty. Elizabeth's understandings about human relationships challenge Anthony's knowledge of basketball—insights that the book supports, which, invariably, shake Ethan's notions of competition and cooperation. Together, the three of them are figuring it out. They not only make their way through the text, but each brings assets to this small community, where they learn to trust one another and their common or divergent lived experiences.

Did you happen to notice they were also engaging with standards? Can you believe these students are enrolled in what the federal government considers a low-income school? Does it surprise you that they are not part of homogeneous learning communities? Are you shocked that the tests identify them as accelerated or advanced readers, but they have never done test prep in their classrooms? Is this possible? We say yes. Teachers can use the workshop methods across a series of instructional contexts from whole-class novels to small reading communities and independent reading to build trust with their students in the process of "humanistic" education (Freire, 1970/1993, p. 75). In doing this, students can experience the standards in dynamic ways that other instruction struggles to cover. They are confident readers, and as a result, the tests do little to shake that confidence.

FINAL THOUGHTS

What we advocate for in the high school English classroom is not complicated. What it requires is for teachers to step out from behind the barrage of testing materials and deficit talk about students, and take stock of the people in front of them.

In further chapters we will talk about our classrooms, located in urban schools and with a rich diversity of class, race, and experiences. Our mixed methods classrooms share a common trait with other models of workshops: They build on trusting what our students bring to the classroom as readers, writers, and, most important, as fellow human beings. Instead of depositing information into the bodies in our classrooms through scripted curricula and test preparation practices, we advocate a curriculum that shares the uncovering of the human experience through literature; one that shapes a new and resilient critical consciousness for our 21st-century students, who are undeniably living on the brink of a global world wholly unlike the one of our adolescence.

Extend Your Thinking

Although humanistic education sounds wonderful, the concept is worthless if teachers cannot put it into practice in their *own* contexts. So, we'd like to offer an opportunity for you to consider the ideas of this chapter as they might apply to your current or future high school English classroom. Before you get started, however, we invite you to think about the students you teach. They are most likely different people than our students, so we'd like to call on you to do some investigative work. These questions will help you tailor our ideas to fit the needs in your classroom:

- What do you know about your students?
- What patterns do they gravitate toward in your classroom?
- What are their interests outside of school?
- What do they know about you?

As you think about these questions, create a t-chart that records how the world has changed since you were a teenager. This will help you further develop your reading curriculum to meet the needs of students who need a critical consciousness for *this* world. How could your literature curriculum reflect that?

Reflecting on what you've learned in this chapter and your answers to the above queries, think of an independent learner, a competitive learner, and a social learner who claimed to hate reading for school. For each student, come up with an idea of how you could

- tap into his or her intrinsic motivation to learn;
- ensure that classroom reading has personal relevance; and
- encourage autonomy to pursue reading for a variety of purposes.

As you finish this activity, talk to your students about where they see themselves in 5 or 10 years. Consider how your reading curriculum could help them construct the kinds of knowledge that will help them in this goal:

- How could it help them make fulfilling choices, communicate tenaciously, express their opinions, and gain results?
- How can it help them listen more effectively and genuinely internalize the ideas of others, separate people from their opinions in a disagreement?
- Will they learn how to resolve conflict respectfully and equitably, use technology in creative and innovative ways, and be prepared for all the dynamic changes their lives will hold?

We believe that you will gain answers to some of these questions as you learn more about our curriculum, but some of your answers will come from conclusions you draw as you read. Make a note to come back to this section and answer these questions as you work your way through the book.

Getting Started with the I Choose, You Choose Curriculum

Photo by Michael Smyth

Because the I Choose, You Choose curriculum offers teachers and students opportunities to co-learn and co-teach, the power that the traditional "banking system" of education holds becomes obsolete in this context (Freire, 1970/1993, p. 75). Instead, this curriculum allows teachers and students to share power, but because it can mean a radical shift in dynamics, we should proceed in stages.

By beginning with the whole-class text (teacher choice), teachers can plan activities that will engage students in decisions regarding assignments, offer them opportunities to learn about working productively in small reading communities, and give them space to explore their thoughts in seminar. All of these activities allow teachers to find out who their students are and what they gravitate toward individually and as a group (Freire, 1970/1993). These activities also help us move into thematic book groups (Chapter 5) and independent reading (Chapter 6) because they establish the framework for more student choice and autonomy.

Classrooms are microcommunities: There are formal and informal leaders; continuous negotiations about purpose, method, and control; and an underlying "life" that can take over the group if not continually analyzed. In learning environments that promote student and teacher choice, such as the I Choose, You Choose curriculum, there are bound to be periods of negotiation. In *From Childhood to Adolescence*, Maria Montessori (1948/1992) writes that high school students are just emerging into their most social period. This period coincides with a period of active brain growth. Bryan Kolb (2000) denotes that this growth occurs through experimental forays into rebellion, group connection, and authority; it is an adolescent's experience that changes the makeup of the brain itself, all the way into adulthood. The methods in the upcoming chapters give high school students opportunities to thrive on their own terms and tap into their desires to experiment as a part of a social learning group; they are offered a safe space for growth as they experience literature. Nevertheless, there will be periods of teacher-student negotiation; we believe, however, that these periods are critical elements for the high school classroom. They are age-appropriate and they move teachers away from banking concepts of education.

We've learned many of our negotiating lessons the hard way: by experience, research, plenty of mistakes, and reflection. Throughout this book, it is important to think about the power shift that will occur in the classroom as you begin sharing the curriculum with high school students. To begin this reflection, we'd like you to think about your best group experience. (This experience could be classroom-based, family-based, work-related, or other.) Then consider the following:

- List the adjectives and images that come to mind when you remember that experience.
- Describe one to two key moments in the formation/follow-through of that group that helped it to succeed.

We would argue that high-functioning groups display certain positive patterns of interaction. They allow members to share power, but also validate each individual.

- What are the key patterns you uncovered about the group experience?
- Now brainstorm three to five ways you could proactively introduce some of these patterns into your own classroom.

Remember these patterns as you plan your curriculum and negotiate power within your own classroom.

PLANNING FOR THE I CHOOSE, YOU CHOOSE CURRICULUM

When you begin the process of shared learning, your job as a teacher will be to make some key structural decisions. Establishing the daily and yearly calendar, learning goals related to the amount of reading and knowledge of reading standards, classroom environment, and behavioral parameters are all within your initial purview. The process can be complicated, so having an overarching but flexible annual plan can help teachers, students, parents, and administrators understand the big picture. In an optimal situation, the entire English department could collaborate to create a coordinated 4-year thematic approach to English.

Developing Guiding Questions

Central to this approach is creating a series of four guiding questions that tie to adolescent developmental stages. These guiding questions become smaller sub-questions as students move through cycles (whole-class text study, thematic book groups, and independent reading) in the I Choose, You Choose curriculum.

Over the past 2 decades, research on adolescence has expanded to include more of a focus on middle and late adolescence and, more important, on the "development of self-conceptions" (Steinberg & Morris, 2001, p. 92). The definition of self-concept comes from a developing awareness of personal beliefs and values. This coincides with an increasingly global self-awareness that directly competes with an effort to understand the self in particular contexts (athletics, peer groups, appearance, and moral conduct) (Steinberg & Morris, 2001).

In our high school, we had the opportunity to work together and plan a 4-year I Choose, You Choose curriculum. We tried to pair our four guiding questions (one for each grade level) with the emerging research on adolescent development. In our department, we used the following four questions:

1. Who am I right now? (year 1—grade 9) (*personal beliefs and values*)
2. How do I define ethnicity and individuality? (year 2—grade 10) (*global self*)
3. What is the relationship between whole and part/society and individual? (year 3—grade 11) (*particular contexts*)
4. What can I contribute to the world? (year 4—grade 12) (*moral conduct*)

In addition to basing our questions on current adolescent research, we also considered patterns we observed among the adolescents in our classrooms. As a result, our questions changed as our students changed throughout the years. This offered more opportunities for departmental collaboration. Although optimally these questions build on one another, they can be used in isolated years if teachers do not have the capacity to plan as departments. We invite you to think about your own structural limitations as you begin planning your curriculum:

- Do you have the ability to plan a 1-, 2-, 3-, or 4-year unit?
- What big questions would you like to pursue with your own students?

Developing Sub-Questions

We always began with that year's guiding question. We paired that question with an initial whole-class text. During that work, we observed patterns in student-led seminar topics, journals, role-plays, and small reading communities. We took note of particular themes our students gravitated toward and used those themes to create our sub-questions for the year. In Figure 3.1, we show you how the overarching guiding question can also serve as the sub-question for quarter one, and lead to other sub-questions throughout the year. Now, look over the guiding questions you have created and perform the following steps:

- Choose one question that would serve as a developmentally appropriate guiding question for your chosen grade level.
- To practice, devise three sub-questions that might be explored as a result of this guiding question (remember, we usually choose these after we've worked through the guiding question with students during quarter 1)

Figure 3.1. Example of a Guiding Question and Sub-Questions

	Quarter	Sub-Questions
Guiding Question Year 2 (Grade 10) How do I define ethnicity and individuality?	1	How do I define ethnicity and individuality?
	2	Is my voice really my own?
	3	Can people collectively use their voices to facilitate change?
	4	What are the societal pressures that inhibit me from using my voice?

Figure 3.2 shows how our text choices align with sub-questions for grade 10. Although we use novels, you can also use this figure as a guide to incorporate whole-class novels, plays, or nonfiction works each quarter that might offer a fruitful experience for you and your students to explore your questions.

Now that you've seen our list, go back to your guiding question and the practice sub-questions you devised.

- Accounting for district reading lists and the age(s) of your students, select a whole-class piece that you believe corresponds with your guiding question.
- What other texts might you cover in conjunction with the sub-questions you chose to follow that initial text?

You've identified a guiding question and practice sub-questions for the year; you've selected your first whole-class reading and possible subsequent texts, and you're ready to begin. You might be starting to envision a balanced workshop/whole-class text approach. Except for one small detail—how will you ever get all of this done?

PUTTING IT ALL TOGETHER

The sections that follow demonstrate how we used the I Choose, You Choose curriculum. The first section outlines a 1-year, 10th-grade I Choose, You Choose curriculum and a 2-year, 11th/12th-grade I Choose, You Choose looping curriculum. The second section discusses how to build these curricula into a 4-year I Choose, You Choose curriculum. We hope you will use the examples as guides rather than prescriptions. In our classrooms, we changed readings and guiding questions annually based on the individuals we worked with, so we advocate fluidity in creating the I Choose, You Choose curriculum.

1- and 2-Year I Choose, You Choose Curricula

The 1-year curriculum is based on the guiding question, sub-questions, and novels introduced in Figure 3.2. Figure 3.3 shows our plan for a 1-year (10th grade) I Choose, You Choose curriculum. Figure 3.4 shows an example of a 2-year (11/12th grade) I Choose, You Choose curriculum. Both figures (presented in an appendix at the end of this chapter) show at a glance how students move through developmentally appropriate and complex sets of

Figure 3.2. Year 1 Texts Paired with Sub-Questions

Quarter	Example Sub-Questions	Novels
1	How do I define ethnicity and individuality?	*The House on Mango Street* by Sandra Cisneros (1991)
2	Is my voice really my own?	*Narrative of the Life of Frederick Douglass* by Frederick Douglass (1845/2008)
3	Can people collectively use their voices to facilitate change?	*Silent Spring* by Rachel Carson (1962/2002)
4	What are the societal pressures that inhibit me from using my voice?	*The Great Gatsby* by F. Scott Fitzgerald (1925/2004)

inquiries, readings, assignments, and learning as they relate to literature. We believe that teachers and students must co-create their learning experiences, and so we suggest that you use these charts to develop your own specific curriculum. In Figure 3.3, we left space for you to imagine how the specific assignments might lead to student learning. In Figure 3.4, we left space for you to create assignments that might lead to the learning described.

In both figures, you can see that reading and writing are inseparable. We pair each whole-class text with a genre of writing that allows students to further explore the sub-question. For example, in Figure 3.3, when students read *The Great Gatsby*, they used the reader response model to produce analysis essays. This pushed them to further investigate thematic underpinnings in the novel. The understanding of Fitzgerald's themes then contributed to their reading experiences with the chosen books from that quarter and ultimately allowed them to choose an audience and topic for the other writing project they engaged in during that quarter, writing business letters.

In a 9-week cycle, we typically began with a teacher-chosen whole-class text (I Choose) and worked on the writing pieces simultaneously, then we moved to the student-chosen (You Choose) piece with book groups, then back to the I Choose piece with short stories, speeches, or a play. We ended the quarter with independent reading. These cycles worked for our students because, at the beginning of the year, we introduced them to independent reading by using the whole-class text study and book groups to guide them through several elements of a trust-based reading curriculum. Equally, because we revisited these cycles throughout the year, students and teacher had equity in choice of literature and activities, further scaffolding with difficult texts or activities, and additional trust-building opportunities. By implementing a diverse set of titles that stem from a guiding question, we could better engage students on a variety of levels in the classroom and, as their personal reading identities developed, their inquiries and independent reading lists expanded throughout the year.

The 4-Year Curriculum

In an optimal situation, a teacher might have the opportunity to plan a 4-year I Choose, You Choose reading curriculum with colleagues in a department. Earlier, we briefly discussed how that was done in our context by choosing an overarching guiding question for each year and then relying on individual grade levels to choose sub-questions with student data. We believe, however, for this book to reach several different types of teachers, it was best to show examples of 1-year and 2-year models, as those are easier to attain if teachers or departments are just beginning to adopt the I Choose, You Choose curriculum. From either of these places, teachers can easily build into a 4-year curriculum. We believe schools should strive for such models. They honor the adolescent by implementing four overarching questions, each pertaining to the developmental needs and interests of a specific grade level; in addition, these 4-year models build on yearly learning, inviting students to make connections across texts, time, and critical points in their independent and academic reading. In addition, cooperative cycles model collaboration among teachers, co-investigation, and the sharing of literature for students.

BUILDING FOUNDATIONS OF TRUST IN THE
I CHOOSE, YOU CHOOSE CURRICULUM

In order to better understand the nature of the micro-community that has formed, it is essential that teachers learn to read their classrooms. This might take the form of taking the daily "status of the class" as Atwell (1998) suggests in her workshop model. It might be a gathering of observational data as is promoted in teacher-research approaches, or it might follow a more tightly-focused survey approach either created at the classroom level or like those found in the Tripod method, part of the Measuring Teacher Effectiveness (MET) Project started in 2010 by the Gates Foundation. The Tripod surveys ask questions across three domains: content, pedagogy, and relationships between teachers and students. We have used a combination of checklists, observations, and informal surveys to understand what our students need. Nevertheless, we found that one of the best ways to gather data about our students at the beginning of the year is to tie whole-class reading to writing projects that nudge them toward close readings and personal reflections.

As an initial trust-building project, we have used Lynda Kale's *Mango books* to build the reading writing connection with the whole-class text study of *The House on Mango Street* by Sandra Cisneros (1991). Kale first implemented the project with 8th-graders at an urban and low-income public school; in 10th grade, however, the project requires some tweaking to better align it with 10th-grade reading standards. Kale begins the project by giving her students a cutout of a shield and asking them to fill in the shield based on what it is they show the world. We give students a piece of paper and foil. We then have them use the foil to create a mirror and the paper to write reflections on what they see when they look in the mirror. This activity allows students to choose what they wish to share with us at the onset of the year.

As we read *The House on Mango Street,* students reflect about main character Esperanza's experiences through student-led seminars, journal writing, and small reading communities. We also teach several mini-lessons on poetic techniques that can be found in the text. Students then practice with these techniques in informal short poetic story (vignette) writing about their lives. Finally, we ask students to choose five vignettes from their informal writing to finalize and publish in a book of their own. They model each after Cisneros' work and implement simile, rhyme, onomatopoeia, symbolism, metaphor, narrative strategies, and a whole host of other techniques in their writings.

Ultimately, we teach students how to construct a book and bind it using only found objects. When we use found objects, we nudge students to create works in an equitable way, without heading off to the craft store to buy their materials. The outside of the cover is the mirror; the inside of the book holds their first writings: an acknowledgments page, table of contents, and their vignettes. On the outside of the cover they visually demonstrate (through collage and artwork) what they show the world about themselves. On the inside, they visually demonstrate what they keep hidden from the world.

The *Mango books* project is one example of how we can open our classrooms at the beginning of the year to the I Choose, You Choose Model and build the reading writing connection. This project allows students to show us who they are and what they are comfortable with in their own literacies. *The House on Mango Street,* although not demanding, is full of nuances and opportunities to delve deeper. By connecting it to a larger writing project that taps into personal experiences, students must read and reread the text carefully.

By reviewing student writing, we also become familiar with struggles they may have with the standards. For example, detecting symbolism, point of view, flashback, simile, and metaphor might be easy for 10th-graders. However, understanding how these writing techniques further author's purpose and affect mood, tone, and setting can be difficult. Teacher-student dialogue helps to draw conclusions about how Cisneros' narration works in parts and with the text as a whole. These prove to be valuable turning points in students' own writing processes, but they also help teachers observe what students might continually struggle with as the year progresses. Working on the books together helps a teacher collect data on students' diverse experiences, range of abilities, and comfort levels with various learning environments.

FINAL THOUGHTS

Finally, and this is by far the most difficult step, leave plenty of space in your ongoing I Choose, You Choose planning for student input. From your students' perspectives, what have been their best classroom experiences? What specific words describe those experiences? What curricular opportunities allowed for these great classroom experiences? How do these connect with who they are and where they are going as readers? Through our *Mango books* project, we discovered that our students were interested in their evolving identities, how these identities were further defined by ethnicities and families, and the struggles people encounter when they work together as change agents in their schools, families, communities, or in our larger society. We then used these observations to choose their novel lists for book groups that year.

Extend Your Thinking

The I Choose, You Choose curriculum allows students to work together, alone, and alongside us. It also offers us opportunities to use this work as a place to learn about student behavior, negotiate parameters, offer opportunities for self-correction, and better understand how we communicate guidelines for our time together. We invite you to think about these ideas as they pertain to your own classroom:

1. What would you like to discover about your students at the beginning of a year?
2. How can you implement the reading and writing connection on an initial project similar to *Mango books*?
3. What would a project like this offer you in planning your I Choose, You Choose curriculum?
4. Revisit your practice sub-questions. Now that you've thought about a possible project, how might those sub-questions change as a result of enacting that project in your classroom?

We encourage you to clearly outline your expectations in the initial trust-building project and throughout the I Choose, You Choose curriculum, but also maintain some flexibility for two-way dialogues. Use the projects, mini-lessons, and reading to establish a predictable pattern in your classroom so students can better understand what you expect and what you will negotiate.

Figure 3.3. 1-Year, 10th-Grade I Choose, You Choose Curriculum

Topic	Titles	Writing Projects	Possible Learning Highlights
Grade 10 (Year 2) Guiding Question: *How do we define ethnicity and individuality?*			
Quarter 1 Sub-Question: *How do I define ethnicity and individuality?*			
Teacher choice: Novel	*The House on Mango Street* by Sandra Cisneros (1991)	Narrative Writing: Mango Books	
Student choice: Narrative writing books	*Step from Heaven*, An Na (2003) *Caramelo*, Sandra Cisneros (2003) *Parrot in the Oven*, Victor Martinez (2004) *My Name is Asher Lev*, Chaim Potok (1972/2003) *My Antonia*, Willa Cather (1918/1994) *Jaguar: A Story of Africans in America*, Paul Stoller (1999)	Narrative Writing: Character monologues Character journal entries Character letter writing	
Teacher choice: Short stories	"Black Women and the Wilderness," Evelyn White (1995) *Flannery O'Connor: Collected Works* (1988) "Erdkinder," Maria Montessori (1948/1992) *Complete Stories and Poems of Edgar Allan Poe* (1984)		
Student choice: Independent reading	Student choice	Journals to partner and teacher (see Atwell, 2007)	
Quarter 2 Sub-Question: *Is my voice really my own?*			
Teacher choice: Classic literature	*Narrative of the Life of Frederick Douglass*, Frederick Douglass (1845/2008)	Informational Essay / Research: Individuals who are/have been change agents	
Student choice: Individuals as change agents	*They Poured Fire on Us From the Sky: The True Story of Three Lost Boys from Sudan*, Alephonsion Deng et al. (2006) *I Know Why the Caged Bird Sings*, Maya Angelou (1969/2009) *All Over But the Shoutin'*, Rick Bragg (1998) *Soul on Ice*, Eldridge Cleaver (1968/1999) *Girl, Interrupted*, Susanna Kaysen (1994) *Summers with the Bears: Six Seasons in the North Woods*, Jack Becklund (1999) *Within Reach: My Everest Story*, Mark Pfetzer and Jack Galvin (2000) *In These Girls, Hope is a Muscle*, Madeleine Blais (1996) *Sugar in the Raw*, Rebecca Carroll (1997) *To Be Young, Gifted, and Black*, Lorraine Hansberry (1969/2011)	Informational Essay / Research: Individuals who are/have been change agents	

Teacher choice: Short stories & essays	Selected speeches of Martin Luther King Jr., Harvey Milk, Angela Davis, Jane Addams, and Gloria Anzaldúa.	Informational Essay/Research: Individuals who are/have been change agents
Student choice: Independent reading	Journals to partner and teacher (see Atwell, 2007)	
Quarter 3 Sub-Question: Can people collectively use their voices to impact change?		
Teacher choice: Full-length nonfiction	*Silent Spring*, Rachel Carson (1962/2002)	Persuasive Writing
Student choice: Narratives of change	*The Awakening*, Kate Chopin (1899/2011) *The Fire Next Time*, James Baldwin (1964/1992) *Autobiography of Malcolm X*, Alex Haley (1965/2010) *The River Why*, David James Duncan (1983/2002) *A River Runs Through It*, Norman MacLean (1976/2001)	Persuasive speeches
Teacher choice: Classic drama	*Romeo and Juliet*, William Shakespeare (1597/1992)	
Student choice: Independent reading	Any	Journals to partner and teacher (see Atwell, 2007)
Quarter 4 Sub-Question: What are the societal pressures that inhibit me from using my voice?		
Teacher choice: Classic literature	*The Great Gatsby* by F. Scott Fitzgerald (1925/2004) (See Chapter 4)	Reader response: analysis
Student choice: Persuasive non-fiction	*Fast Food Nation*, Eric Schlosser (2001) *The Things They Carried*, Tim O'Brien (1990) *The Joy Luck Club*, Amy Tan (1989) *Native Son*, Richard Wright (1940/1996)	Business letters
Student choice	*Fahrenheit 451*, Ray Bradbury (1953/1987) *Sacred Hoops*, Phil Jackson and Hugh Delehanty (1995) *The Bean Trees*, Barbara Kingsolver (1988/2009) *A Wizard of Earthsea*, Ursula Le Guin (1968/2004)	
Student choice: Independent reading	Any	Journals to partner and teacher (see Atwell, 2007)

Figure 3.4. 2-Year, 11th-/12th-Grade I Choose, You Choose Curriculum

Topic	Titles	Student Learning Highlights	Possible Projects
Year One (Grade 11) Guiding Question: What is the relationship between whole and part/society and individual?			
Teacher chooses: Summer reading—multiple narrators	*Extremely Loud and Incredibly Close*, Jonathan Safran Foer (2006)	Powerful response to 9/11, a historical event that has shaped our students' lives / Exploring the power of invention and imagination in our lives	
Students choose: Summer reading—multiple narrators	*Flight*, Sherman Alexie (2007); *Dracula*, Bram Stoker (1897/2000); *The Moonstone*, Wilkie Collins (1868/2003); *The Pact: Three Young Men Make a Promise and Fulfill a Dream*, Sampson Davis et al. (2003); *The Bluest Eye*, Toni Morrison (1970/2000); *The Poisonwood Bible*, Barbara Kingsolver (1998/2003)	Synthesizing varying voices into a unifying theme	
Students choose: Social Action Plays	*The Crucible*, Arthur Miller (1953/2003); *The Laramie Project*, Moises Kaufman (2001); *Threepenny Opera*, Bertold Brecht (1928/2007)	Public speaking & performance / Central metaphors that awaken deeper understanding	
Teacher chooses: Classic literature	*The Three Theban Plays: Antigone; Oedipus the King; Oedipus at Colonus*, Sophocles (1982/2000)	Mastery of an ancient text / Depth & ubiquity of sight/blindness metaphors	
Students choose: Dystopia / Sci-Fi	*The Handmaid's Tale*, Margaret Atwood (1985/2006); *Brave New World*, Aldous Huxley (1932/1998); *Parable of the Sower*, Octavia Butler (1993/2000)	Historical/sociological awareness / Seek out positive contributions to the world	
Teacher chooses: Classic literature	*Hamlet*, William Shakespeare (1603/2003)	Power of individual character / Complexity of characters / Mastery of one of literature's great plays	
Students choose: Gender/Race *students read a book they self-identify with their own gender/race identity.	*Jane Eyre*, Charlotte Bronte (1864/2011); *Death of a Salesman*, Arthur Miller (1949/1998); *Soul on Ice*, Eldridge Cleaver (1968/1999); *Caucasia*, Danzy Senna (1999)	Power of reading about one's identity with others who share that identity	
Teacher chooses: contemporary classic	*Song of Solomon*, Toni Morrison (1977/1987)	Adaptability of metaphors to life situations / Every student finds him/herself in text / Epic themes feel close to home / Stunning passages speak the truth	

Students choose: "Great reads"	*Catcher in the Rye*, J. D. Salinger (1951/2001) *Sula*, Toni Morrison (1973/1982) *Angels in America*, Tony Kushner (1993) *Ten Little Indians*, Sherman Alexie (2003)	Pleasure of reading Sharing books with others Trust that new books can be great reads
Year Two (Grade 12) Guiding Question: What can I contribute to the world?		
Students choose: Summer reading—individual reading lists (see Chapter 6)	Thousands of choices, each student identifying a list of books centered on a "unifying element" that appeals to their sense of self, intellect, curiosity, and engagement.	Life-long development of readers Trust between students and teacher
Teacher chooses: New York poetry	Selected poems by Walt Whitman and Saul Williams	Power of poetry Rhetorical analysis of syntax and rhythm Inspiration for college essays
Students choose	Independent book #1	Emerging self-reliance Trust in self to engage with material to complete external standards
Teacher chooses: Classic drama	*Othello*, William Shakespeare (1622/2004)	Power of seeing how doing good for one's self can put harm into the world
Students choose	Independent book #2	Continuing self-reliance Joining a scholarly community at university level
Teacher chooses: Classic literature	Selections from *Walden*, Henry David Thoreau (1854/1995) & selected essays by Ralph Waldo Emerson	Working with hands to build a strong shelter Metaphor of shelter and protection Tenets of transcendentalism and self-reliance
Students choose	Independent book #3	Increased confidence in reading skill Increased trust in teacher as guide and peers as intellectual community members
Teacher chooses: Modern literature	*Invisible Man*, Ralph Ellison (1953/1995) (See Chapter 4)	Power of light/cave metaphor Inspiring others to act by coming into the light
Students choose	Independent book #4	Satisfaction in having developed own list Mastery of all district/common core literary standards Presumption of lifelong literacy
Students and Teacher choose: Great Books—Nobel, Pulitzer, Booker prize winners (note: students nominate texts and I choose from experience)	*The Unbearable Lightness of Being*, Milan Kundera (1984/1999) *Beloved*, Toni Morrison (1987/1998) *One Hundred Years of Solitude*, Gabriel García Márquez (1967/1998) *Crime and Punishment*, Fyodor Dostoevsky (1886/1996) *Confederacy of Dunces*, John Kennedy Toole (1980/1994)	Students learn the tenants of the literary cannon, how it's chosen, and what that means for them as individuals and readers.

CHAPTER 4

Trust Me! I Can Teach
Revisiting the Whole-Class Text

Photo by Michael Smyth

Building trust across the boundaries of personal taste and external mandates pervades the American school experience. It is not our job as English teachers to make our students love each book that we present to them. It is our job to teach them to use their minds in the service of becoming literate beings—readers who can engage with a text through its message, craft, and cultural contributions.

Spending time with a whole-class text need not negate individuality just because you're reading it together; in fact, it can serve to emphasize the fruitful individuality that grows from a collective reading experience. Nel Noddings (1992) writes that "part of what children need to learn is that groups need not be accepted or rejected wholly" (p. 54). Opportunities to choose sides socially, politically, religiously, and culturally surround young people daily. Our classrooms can be spaces for students to evaluate individuals, rather than the groups they identify with, contexts where they find commonalities with those of different groups and are sometimes challenged by those they consider part of their group. When we assign a whole-class text, we build trust with our students by making that text part of a greater strategy to foster each student's sense of herself as an individual, a literate being, and a member of a diverse group of people.

However, opening these spaces can be difficult when we must teach a text that the district has assigned, rather than one of our own choosing. Our strategy is to work to find what richness the communal reading experience might offer, even when the text itself is challenging for us. Whether you are required to teach a specific whole-class text or are fortunate enough to choose your own, it is essential that you use the experience to both help build a trusting community of literate beings and teach each student that he is capable of being a strong, independent reader and thinker.

ESTABLISHING METHODOLOGICAL FOUNDATIONS WITH WHOLE-CLASS TEXTS

Through our practice, we found a core group of methods that help initiate trusting experiences in our classrooms. We implement these methods with the whole-class text and further their use throughout our I Choose, You Choose curriculum. We discuss each method in the following sections. You will see these methods used throughout our discussions in the following chapters.

Guiding Questions

Guiding questions are the open-ended, unanswerable questions that guide our readings. Alfred Tatum (2009) calls these "essential questions" and defines them as questions that ask "educators and students to engage in dialogue about issues or concepts that matter to school and society" (p. 91). Allowing students to grapple with the big questions that we often still wonder about builds on our shared mission and furthers trusting practices. Remember, we choose these questions for our students based on patterns they exhibit as individuals and themes they seem to gravitate toward as we read. We design the questions so they can be explored, not answered, by our classroom community. Sometimes, the questions create conflict or discomfort for us, but they help us engage with texts in personally and socially relevant ways (Tatum, 2009). We outlined the guiding questions and sub-questions for our I Choose, You Choose curricula in Figures 3.3 and 3.4.

In our classes, students spend a small informal amount of time each day discussing how the guiding question or sub-question came up in the reading from the night before. They do this in what we call *peer conversations*, which are small dialogues with a neighbor about the question and the reading. These peer conversations help students reorient themselves to the reading before the bigger work of class begins.

Student-Led Seminars

A student-led seminar, sometimes called *Socratic Seminar,* can have varying forms (Elkind & Sweet, 1997; Tredway, 1995). We prefer the term *student-led seminar* to describe what our students did because there was very little teacher direction in the process, as opposed to some forms of Socratic Seminar where teachers play a significant role. Student-led seminars are widely used on the middle- and high-school levels as tools for developing discussions with larger groups. In our classrooms, student-led seminars are another key feature of establishing trust. Students gain new evidence that they have as much claim to building literary and personal meaning as we do.

For our seminars, students often completed seminar preparation tools: short assignments to focus their thoughts for seminar or small reading community discussions. In our classes, seminar preparation tools ranged from letters to characters, artistic responses (drawings, collage, etc.) to specific scenes, character sketches, discussion questions and responses, and double-entry journals or *visual notebooks.* Visual notebooks are journals that students compile as responses to reading. They can include pictures, newspaper or magazine clippings, and their own writing. In a visual notebook, they choose objects from their own lives to portray how a text connects to them personally. Then, in their journal writing, they extend that initial connection in to more complex textual, literary, and global connections. Students completed this assignment for homework or during the first part of class.

Here is one possible format for a student-led seminar:

1. Students and teacher sit in a circle on the floor or in chairs at an equal level (without desks separating them).
2. Students bring to the circle a seminar preparation tool, the text, and something to write with. (Students also may bring clipboards so that they do not have to fumble with binders and notebooks during the seminar. You can make your own clipboards with binder clips and heavy/foam board.)
3. To open the seminar, students share lines from their preparation materials and pose one question to the group regarding that reading. Each share lasts no more than 15 seconds.
4. As each student reads, the other students write his or her name down and a few notes about the question posed.

5. At the end of the readings (about 5 minutes), the teacher opens the discussion for students to begin responding to questions.
6. A student will volunteer. He or she will speak directly to the person (by name) and expand on the question he or she posed. That student will then form another question based on his or her response and pose it to the group.
7. He or she will then call on another classmate by name to answer his or her question.
8. As they share, students can take notes on others' responses and continue to jot down questions. They are also encouraged to use the text specifically (page numbers) to expand on their answers to questions.
9. At the end of the seminar, the teacher gives his or her feedback. (During seminar, we keep a running list of what our contributions would be if we were to speak [we've found that our voices can take over the conversation]. We then frame these comments into what we noticed, what we felt good about, and what we'd like to see improve. In this context, the points we make serve to further students' experiences personally and with the literature.)

The teacher's role during seminar is to listen and take notes. If a teacher wishes to grade seminar, sometimes it's best to grade students using a rubric created by group expectations and district standards. We often look at our collected data across multiple measures: listening and understanding of text, use of text, extensions, focusing on peers, voice quality, building ideas (rather than repeating). Figure 4.1 offers an example of how seminar expectations can be communicated in a trusting classroom.

It is important to note that students need to be able to make choices in seminar based on their current practice. For example, Carl, a former student, states,

Figure 4.1. Student-Led Seminar Expectations

___ (P) The student is prepared with a *preparation* tool, the text, and a writing utensil.
___ (L) The student actively *listens* to the sharing that takes place. This is evident by the note taking he or she displays and eye contact with the speaker.
___ (S) The student *shares* by discussing his or her opinion on the question, using text to expand, and then posing another, related question to the group. The student shows evidence of building on the conversation rather than repeating ideas.
___ (C) The student encourages and fosters *community* by calling respectfully on classmates by their names, not dominating the conversation, agreeing or disagreeing with the position—not the individual.

"Seminar allowed me to see different perspectives, participate, and think in ways I didn't think before." His experience, however, contradicts Amanda, who says, "Speaking in seminar made me uncomfortable and sometimes I didn't feel safe because I was more shy in the beginning of high school." As teachers, we need to honor the students who fit into these categories and all those who fall in between these students' experiences. Options regarding how to show participation can include active listening and note-taking, oral participation, post-seminar reflections, seminar preparation pieces, initial sharing as a whole class, and one-on-one discussions with the teacher after class. On any given day, students may feel more comfortable being vocal or more comfortable listening, taking notes, and handing in their reflections. Each of these methods validates students and helps them feel safer taking risks in other areas of seminar. We encourage students to hand in any materials they wish at the end of the seminar. We then take these materials and use them to help us further assess their performance in the seminar.

Small Reading Communities

Small reading communities are similar to book clubs in the classroom. At the beginning of the quarter, we place students in a community based on their responses to the brief survey shown in Figure 4.2.

Students are generally honest, respectful, and thoughtful in these responses, and we trust that they will be. From these surveys, we choose their reading communities for the quarter.

In this meeting time, students might share a preparation tool, work together on an ongoing project involving the novel, or get feedback from one another on individual work they are doing in relation to the text. Although we set the foundation for these groups during whole-class texts, we see small reading communities as opportunities for students to practice their group dynamics before they begin working in the book groups we discuss in Chapter 5. Because they understand the patterns in small reading communities, the transition to choosing books as a group and then building discussions around these texts becomes much easier for students.

Mini-lessons

Mini-lessons, developed by Nancie Atwell (1998), are very short (10 to 20 minutes) lessons that range in topics. We choose mini-lesson topics based on what we observe our students struggling with in seminars, in their reading communities, and in their homework. Topics might include introducing and evaluating literary elements, tackling difficult passages, lessons on how to discuss in small or large groups, or tips on writing discussion questions.

Figure 4.2. Student Survey Questions

1. What kinds of reading have you been doing lately (novels, Internet, text messaging, social networks, poetry, magazines, etc.)?
2. In what ways do you share your reading with others (reading together, talking to parents or friends)?
3. What do you think a good conversation feels like?
4. Is there anyone in the class you would prefer to be in a group with? (I will do my best to honor your choice.) Why?
5. Is there anyone in the class whom you prefer not to work with?

Please be aware your responses are confidential. I use them only to help choose your group for your small reading community.

Mini-lessons always incorporate a short amount of time for students to practice a new skill together. We provide direct focused instruction for 1 to 5 minutes, and then we let students practice the new material while we walk around and coach pairs and groups. It's important to us that they get to the business of *doing* rather than spending too much time receiving information on how to do it. This is how we offer opportunities to make mistakes, self-correct, learn interdependence, and, ultimately help them to do it alone. Often our practice time will involve students using drama, artistic response, text pairings, or writing to engage further with the new skill. Figure 4.3 shows a mini-lesson plan sheet developed by Sally and her colleagues.

Reading Time and Reading Homework

We always allow students time to read during class. High school students' lives are busy. Teachers also need time for individual coaching and class observation. Combining the two shows our students that we trust them to read and they can trust us to attend to their individual learning needs.

We offer a variety of settings for this reading and allow students to choose how they will read (in pairs, silently, as a group, or in the listening center). Because we taught in mixed ability classrooms, these choices were extremely important for our students. Some of them needed to wear headphones and listen to the text, some used e-readers, others needed complete silence, and still others needed to read and process with a trusted peer or small group. All of these scenarios are fine with us. Why? Because each trusts an individual to choose the method that will meet his or her needs on that particular day and each brings us that much closer to having our students choose to read independently.

Also, we did not assign long sections of the text to be read on a given night. Instead, we assigned what was appropriate for the students in our

Figure 4.3. Mini-Lesson Plan Sheet

Topic _____

Preparing the Environment

1. **Context:** Note the grade level and perhaps the specific subject (e.g., American Literature, Advanced Composition).
2. **Broad Lifelong Goal/s & Rationale:** Consider this the "so what" of a mini-lesson. Think about how the lesson will help students become better readers, writers, thinkers, and people outside of school.
3. **Specific Daily Objectives**: Don't state that the objective is to have a discussion; rather, state what the students will have *learned* from having this particular discussion.
4. **State or National Standards**: Be sure to intricately tie these to the daily objectives.
5. **Materials:** Include everything you need to conduct your lesson (e.g., short literary works, handouts, assessment tools, etc.).
6. **Movement:** Consider how students will transition from one activity to the next. What are your expectations for moving around the room, using materials, passing out papers, small group work, etc.? You need to have these in mind and articulate them simply and clearly to students *before* they begin working.

Plan for teaching (remember, your goal here is to gradually help students do the task alone):

Methods/Procedures

Anticipation (3 to 5 minutes): How will you initially and briefly anchor students in the subject matter or activity? This could be through a journal, a series of pictures, a movie clip, and so forth.

Overview and Modeling (3 to 5 minutes): How will you briefly and clearly introduce students to what they will be learning during this lesson? It is important to consider ways of making this portion of the lesson active instead of teacher centered (stations, pictures with captions, a read-aloud are all appropriate activities that introduce students to a topic while still engaging them). You should also plan to model the skill for them during this time. We often learn the definition of a concept by seeing the example.

Guided Practice (5 to 10 minutes): This should be an *experience* in which students work together at trying out new knowledge. You should design this portion of the lesson to be an opportunity for students to manipulate, problem solve, or construct knowledge together with you coaching at a small-group or pair level. The trick here is to have them practice in context—so if they've just learned what flashback is, have them work together to find it in the text they are currently reading.

Closure (3 to 5 minutes): How will you take students back to your objectives and goals? How will you transition them into the activity for the rest of the class?

Created by Sally Lamping, Angela Beumer-Johnson, and Nancy Mack, Wright State University, Dayton, Ohio.

---

class—something that tried to meet them right in the middle. We based this reading pace on data we gleaned from students as we became familiar with their reading practices and got to know how quickly they read and what they read outside of school. We also provided a list of required books with approximate start dates to parents and students at the beginning of the year; this offered students opportunities to start earlier if needed. Because we needed them to read the text, not take shortcuts, we tried to make our assignments doable. If students read more, we asked that they not spoil it for their peers and they honored this request. If students could not meet these requirements, we worked with them, but we refrained from excluding them because they had not read.

It could be said that if students are not reading the text, they could get the answers and fake it by simply participating in class every day. Our former student Carl states that class time allowed him an opportunity for what he called "redemption." He said, "Maybe if I didn't have the opportunity to read all of what I was supposed to read, hearing what others said helped paint a more vivid picture of the book—especially for when I did go back and read." What's important in Carl's statement is that he states explicitly that he did "go back and read." Sometimes, students don't have time to read, but they deserve to continue to be a part of the dialogue surrounding reading. Often, immersion in this dialogue helps nonreaders become readers.

Teachers can do this by making class time so engaging for our readers that they *want* to read each night and feel a responsibility to their peers to read every night. Teachers can rely on the social aspects of classrooms to help students take care of the trusting practices they build with them. Amanda, a former student, remembers, "I didn't want to let anyone down, so I did my work to the best of my ability to keep the trust." We know that these relationships matter to students, so we established environments that helped them succeed with their reading and classroom relationships. Does it work? Yes. We trusted them to read and, in the infrequent occurrence that they didn't, we figured it out, but we didn't exclude them from the valuable conversations and relationships that can come out of reading.

CHOOSING A WHOLE-CLASS TEXT

When given opportunities to choose literature for our students, we want texts that will offer them the following experiences:

1. A chance to explore universal themes across time and contexts.
2. Opportunities to witness complex characters grapple with their actions and reactions to events, society's economic, cultural, and racial influences, and other characters.
3. Invitations to empathize by seeing characters, themes, and events as universal and applicable to their own experiences, even when they offer surface indications that they are far removed from our realities.
4. Layered plots that require us to be vulnerable readers when we move through the complicated elements in the text.
5. A deeper, more nuanced understanding of our common and divergent human experiences.
6. Opportunities to experiment with various styles/levels of decision making and risk taking.

Although we have taught a wide range of texts to entire classes of students and some have been better choices than others, we chose *The Great Gatsby* by F. Scott Fitzgerald (1925/2004) as a Grades 9/10 example and *Invisible Man* by Ralph Ellison (1953/1995) as a Grades 11/12 example in this chapter. Both uphold the six requirements we abide by when choosing texts for our students, and both are novels commonly taught in high school. These texts alone are incredibly complex pieces that invite readers on journeys muddied by economic, racial, and cultural influences. What we hope to offer here is a new way of looking at each that highlights the opportunities they can offer high school students.

Trusting Students to Uncover Complexities in *The Great Gatsby*

The cover of our school edition of *The Great Gatsby* (1925/2004) shows a face rising up above a valley of ashes. It is not particularly interesting to students with no prior knowledge of the text; it does not invite students to read in a memorable way. If we take this a step further and place it in the context of our classrooms, the outside of the book offers nothing to, for example, a Hispanic student growing up in an urban area aside from another opportunity to read about rich White people. Asking ethnically and socioeconomically mixed classrooms of students to go home, read

Chapter 1, and fill out the study guide for the book will not encourage lifelong literacy practices.

Steven Wolk (2009) writes, "While a nation of workers requires a country that *can* read, a democracy requires people that *do* read, read widely, and think and act in response to their reading" (p. 665). Through our experience as teachers and teacher educators, we found that an inordinate amount of time is spent in high school classrooms trying to catch students who are cheating, using online summaries of texts, or downloading papers from the Internet. This is certainly indicative of the societal patterns our schools reinforce—patterns that create graduates who *can* read instead of those who *do* read. So, how do teachers single-handedly conquer this problem? How do they make students into people who *do* read when teachers can't even get them *to* read? Our answer is simple: Place the text at the center of the classroom and allow the author to do the work. Teachers can create the structure within which students can safely explore the text, make choices, test their perceptions, and grapple with the larger issues, all while honoring the text itself and what they, as readers, bring to it. Teachers can offer experiences that ask students to tap into their desires to read attentively.

Guiding Questions that Set the Unit Foundation. *The Great Gatsby* unit example has two guiding sub-questions: What are the societal pressures that inhibit me from using my voice? And, a sub-question that frequently rose out of the previous question, how does money help or hinder us from using our authentic voices? During student-led seminars, small reading communities, and peer conversations, we consistently explored these two questions. So, during a 50-minute class period, we began with a peer discussion over guiding questions (3 to 5 minutes), then, we would have a mini-lesson (10 to 15 minutes). We then moved on to practice the skills students learned in the mini-lesson in small reading communities or in larger seminar (20 to 25 minutes). We allowed them time to read as a class either silently, in pairs, or at the listening stations (10 to 15 minutes) and we closed the class by revisiting the guiding questions and looking forward in the reading (3 to 5 minutes).

Initial Trust Building Mini-Lesson. On the first day of the unit, Sally sets up a table with various objects found in the text (artifacts) for the mini-lesson, while students read the first chapter in class. Initial reading time allows her to gauge how many pages students can read in a given time and the artifacts offer a focal point for initially distracted readers. She asks them to look up during their reading and choose an object that they recognize and believe fits with their ideas about the reading so far.

Whenever they are ready, students can whisper to their partners about the object, and then move quietly to the artifact table and choose an object. In pairs, students then present these objects to the class in short artifact summaries (20 seconds each), when they discuss how the object connects, summarize the part of the text the object is in, or how a character uses it within the text. Sally uses these artifact speeches to illicit responses to more complicated parts of the reading. These simple tangible items help make the initially difficult sections of *The Great Gatsby* more memorable by providing students with safe opportunities to choose responses.

The above mini-lesson trusts students to do what readers do when they struggle with a text: depend on a peer for a deeper understanding of an experience. It also teaches them the independence of making choices and the interdependence required to make inferences from the options provided. It relies on their assets to establish initial connections with the text and trusts them to deconstruct complicated overarching ideas without any initial background lecture on the text.

Alternatives to Nightly Study Guides. For nightly responses to readings, Sally uses a simple character map that includes an outline of a character and directions for filling in the sheet visually and with textual evidence. Students choose one character to follow throughout the novel. On the front side of the sheet, students have a large outline of a person. Each night, they sketch in one of the following on the outline: physical characteristics, expressions, what the character brings to the text (left hand), what the character takes away from the text (right hand), symbols (a torn shirt or a cracked face might show turmoil, a specific color might represent harmony or peace, etc.). On the back of the outline, Sally asks them to write textual evidence in support of each addition they make to the outline and label the evidence accordingly. The outline can be folded and used as a bookmark during reading.

Students should be permitted to experiment with this structure to meet their own artistic and reading needs. Their modifications might include the making of character pop-ups, puppets, collaged artifacts, life-size character maps, character books, and character frames. Sally allowed them to work with the structure of the artistic response as long as they were still adding the pieces she discusses in the assignment's parameters. Sally found that this type of choice within the framework of the assignment helped artistic students use their skills to aid their reading, but it did not add pressure to those who have difficultly drawing.

Unlike a study guide, this activity assumes that students not only *will* read when engaged, but they will also make predictions, pass judgment, uncover subtleties, and analyze motives. All of these are patterns of people who *do* read and react to a text. By the end of the book, the goal is for the students to know and understand the characters intimately. In doing this, they also inadvertently follow the plot and interactions with other characters in the text. Sally incorporates these maps into everyday activities by using them in small reading groups and seminars. Students do this by using their character map as a springboard for writing discussion questions or, in small groups, students might switch maps with a peer and write questions for the map's creators about the choices they made when constructing the map.

Connecting Daily Work to a Culminating Project. Near the end of the reading (specifically when Myrtle is hit by the car), Sally introduces the murder mystery party, which she adapted from some of the framework Ruth Vinz, Erick Gordon, and Bill Lundgren outline for their "Mockingbird Monologues" in *Becoming Other(wise)* (2000). For this project, students use their created character maps as significant aids in developing the persona of a murderer.

On the day after students have read the scene for homework, they re-read the scene as a class mini-lesson, taking note of the nuances in the text and paying close attention to the question "Who killed Myrtle?" Students can interpret this scene in a variety of ways, even down to the idea that Myrtle killed herself or Daisy achieved all of this with purpose. Using their character maps, they create a cover story for their characters. In pairs, they practice their cover story as a response to a specific context. Some examples might be: cheating, money, gender roles, children and families, and control.

On the day of the party, students dress as the character and bring a snack that represents their characters. Students are invited to open the party by introducing themselves and their snacks. Then, Sally invites them to sit at any table with one of the topics (cheating, money, gender roles, children and families, and control) from the day before. There, students find discussion questions relating to the topic and they can use their cover stories to discuss each question with classmates while in character. Sally works as the timekeeper and observer, having students move around the room after about 3 minutes at a table. She sits at each table, keeping time and taking notes on the students who engage in discussion. Ultimately, she observes each student answer questions at a given table. She uses the rest of their cover story and initial introduction to help evaluate overall performance. As these discussions unfold, students use tally sheets to track their conversations with other guests in hopes of finding the actual murderer.

Finally, Sally collects all of their cover stories and offers feedback. Students then use these materials and feedback to help them construct their Gatsby analysis papers later in the quarter.

Using Living Metaphors to Explore *Invisible Man*

Dean teaches Ralph Ellison's (1953/1995) *Invisible Man* at the 12th-grade level, about three quarters of the way through the year, after her students have had considerable experience connecting big themes with specific text. *Invisible Man* offers an incredible array of literary richness, universal themes, and appealing story lines for students. Its flexibility stems from the multiple layers with which individuals can read it. Most of all, its wide variety of strong metaphors, serve as strong models for the culminating assignment: the living metaphor museum.

Analyzing the Use of Metaphor. Dean's class reads the novel together, using activities similar to Sally's in that they focus on student responses and analysis of the texts, but extend, deepen and build upon their work with literature. At the heart of the unit, students identify a metaphor from the novel that in some way speaks to them, and then write a short essay that analyzes Ellison's use of the metaphor. When the final assessment comes close, they re-read Ellison's (1953/1995) description of his hiding room:

> My hole is warm and full of light. Yes, *full* of light. I doubt if there is a brighter spot in all New York than this hole of mine, and I do not exclude Broadway. Or the Empire State Building on a photographer's dream night. . . . That is why I fight my battle with Monopolated Light & Power. The deeper reason, I mean: It allows me to feel my vital aliveness. I also fight them for taking so much of my money before I learned to protect myself. In my hole in the basement there are exactly 1369 lights. I've wired the entire ceiling, every inch of it. . . . Though invisible, I am in the great American tradition of tinkers. That makes me kin to Ford, Edison and Franklin. Call me, since I have a theory and a concept, a "thinker-tinker." Yes, I'll warm my shoes; they need it, they're usually full of holes. I'll do that and more. (p. 5)

Students work with photocopies of the excerpt, underlining key images and brainstorming thematic connections in the margins. Having finished the book, the lightbulb room Ellison describes is not only clearer, but takes on new meaning for the students. They better understand the power of the light imagery, the implications of power, and the "realness" of this previously shadowy room.

Building a Living Metaphor Museum. After a discussion of the students' findings, Dean announces the final assessment task of the unit: Each student must conceive of a living metaphor that captures a profound truth of their lives, and then physically build (either full-scale or model size) the object to be displayed in a museum of metaphors.

Dean emphasizes the importance of using available materials. No student should have to go out and buy extra materials—part of the exercise is to emulate Ellison: to become a thinker-tinker, and to bring together objects from their lives into a central metaphor that can explore some intricacy of their personhood. She tells students to keep a piece of paper handy for when inspiration strikes. Some students are immediately inspired by this project, and can draw on complexities of their lives to create an image. Others need more guidance.

On the second day of the project, Dean asks them to identify something about themselves that causes them distress, or joy, or exhilaration, or pain—something worthy of further exploration. She guides them through a series of brainstorming and drawing exercises, moving them into increasingly concrete ideas that can yield metaphoric richness. Some students return to their college application essays (an essay they work on throughout their junior year) and further their ideas. Others talk with their best friends or with family members for ideas. By the third day of the project, however, they each commit to an idea and begin to build the physical aspect of the metaphor.

Presenting Living Metaphors. On the day of the museum exhibition, students arrive early to store their work in the classroom. Students set out their creations, and write a brief museum card with the title, artist, materials, and a brief blurb about its meaning. Silently, students move through the museum, carefully examining their peers' work, and documenting their findings on an interpretation sheet. After 20 to 30 minutes, they gather together in a circle for an artist's talk. During this activity, students can talk with each other about what they have seen. It is in this moment that the collective trust-building bears real fruits.

Students freely share their own intentions in creating personal living metaphors, but beyond that, their peers extend additional insights. For example, one student, David, created a tuxedo entirely from silver duct tape. His blurb stated that he enjoyed the irony of making a fancy garment out of cheap materials. During the artist's talk, one of his peers pointed out that his choice of duct tape also might mean that he was in fact protecting himself—that the tuxedo looked like a suit of armor. David's response was visible: His face brightened and relaxed as his fellow student went on to say that it was important for everyone to have protections for themselves. Denisha covered a Barbie doll entirely with red clay, etching intricate patterns into the skin, and replacing the head with an eyeless, mouthless ovoid. Her artist's blurb read that she felt simultaneously indistinguishable from others (hence the Barbie) and individual (hence the patterns), and that the clay was intended to suggest her malleability.

Learning from Living Metaphors. Dean's students learned the visceral importance of metaphors. They understand that a metaphor must be concrete and solid while also being symbolic and universal. They can spot a literary metaphor anywhere (sometimes joking that they see them in real objects outside of books), and also find solace in the idea that the themes of their own lives can become represented externally. These are enormous lessons for students exiting high school to take into adulthood. They extend beyond the basic level of understanding put forth by the Common Core Standards Initiative (2010) for 11th- and 12th-graders, which ask only that students "determine the meaning of words. . . , include figurative or connotative meanings. . . , analyze the impact of specific word choices on meaning and tone, including words with multiple meanings" (p. 38). Asking students to identify with and learn from metaphors creates a base level of curiosity about literary richness from which they can draw throughout their lives. Not only have students learned to trust themselves as readers (having deeply understood what it means to read between the lines), but they have engaged in a trusting relationship with their peers that has led to greater understanding and validation of themselves as individuals.

FINAL THOUGHTS

During whole-class novel study, teachers can offer students experiences that call on them to begin or continue to trust themselves and their classroom communities in their reading practices. The activities described in a 9th/10th-grade and 11th/12th-grade context offer teachers valuable methods for teaching age-appropriate whole-class texts. In addition, they offer a valuable lesson: It is both the text and the experiences surrounding the text that call readers toward trusting practices within their reading.

Extend Your Thinking

A trust-based reading curriculum in a testing-focused educational climate must encompass methods that foster trust in a classroom, inspire critical thinking about literature, and use the standards as a framework for choosing content. At this point, we recommend that you pick a project you've done with students in the past, or one you'd like to try. You could even go back to the text and guiding questions you chose earlier and begin designing a project around that reading. Follow these questions as you map out how you might enact it in your classroom:

1. What standards does the project focus on? Can these standards be tied to any text? If so, which text(s) would work best with your students? If not, what text will you be using?
2. In what ways can you alter this project so students are living the lessons the literature offers? For example, how can you make the project so students have multiple opportunities to try out their learning in real scenarios (not by worksheets, but by using and reflecting on objects and ideas that surround them)?
3. What are the necessary steps to get students from the beginning of this reading project to the end? Write these steps out one by one. If you handed this sheet of steps to students, would they be able to accomplish the end goal with very little help? (That's how you know you have enough steps. We recommend introducing each step to the project as it comes rather than all at once.)
4. Are there opportunities within each step of the project for students to communicate with each other, work on a common goal, work independently, and test their knowledge? If not, how can you incorporate these key trust-building practices?

Trust Us! We Can Learn Together
Transitioning to Thematic Book Groups

Photo by Michael Smyth

T**ARA COMPLAINS THAT HER** 9th-grade students are rambunctious, hate to read, and are incapable of taking novels home without losing them. Her students do all of their reading in class from the literature textbook or from class sets of novels. Due to these patterns, she is absolutely convinced that her students are unable to participate in book groups. In fact, Tara implemented a rewards system for students who successfully stay in their seats until the bell. Trying to imagine them reading in groups, discussing books with their peers, moving about the room, and managing their own time sends her into a panic. This is not to say Tara does not care about her students. In fact, she cares deeply, but considers their boisterous behaviors to be signals to her, as the teacher, to gain more control over their interactions.

In order to have successful book groups, Tara must find a way to tap into the social interaction in her classrooms. She must also discover ways to set parameters for this type of learning and classroom interaction. Beginning book groups with any class requires that we teach students *how* to be with one another (and the teacher) in a socially academic setting. Teachers can begin this process by using small reading communities in conjunction with a whole-class text. Book groups, however, require more power-sharing with students, but the rewards for adolescents are undeniably positive.

Frank Smith (1992) writes that "you learn from the company you keep" (p. 432). Every day, we learn from our social interactions. Why? The spaces within the school when students share meals together, talk, and interact in a purely social fashion tap into their social qualities. If we learn from the company we keep, there is a lot of learning going on at lunchtime.

Lev Vygotsky (1934/1986) believed that social interaction presents us with a wide range of ideas that can cause imbalances in our thinking and push us toward resolve by adopting new ways of thinking, considering alternate viewpoints, and understanding others' experiences. He also noted that it is in adolescence when we begin to regulate our actions through advanced levels of thought. These adolescent social interactions are valuable and sensitive times that help young people learn how to function as citizens of the world. We should create opportunities for young people to practice regulating their actions by considering their peers' experiences and viewpoints. Thematic book groups can provide opportunities for meaningful contextual learning, choice, and collaboration.

Former student Joe's comments on book groups mirror Vygotsky's claims:

> Book groups offered me a different angle on a book that I didn't see before then. They made me feel like I wasn't alone in my interpretations. My group helped me see different perspectives, but also expand what I thought I knew about the book.

Although each student experiences book groups differently, the low-risk, small-group environment provides an excellent space for students to explore reading independence and trusting relationships with one another.

SETTING THE FOUNDATION FOR BOOK GROUPS

Even though book groups can be created at any time, we found they work best after students experience a whole-class text. The whole-class text allows students to experiment with small reading communities, student-led seminar, and personally engaging projects. These methods offer teachers opportunities to observe student dynamics in each setting, student understanding of texts, and any common themes or ideas students gravitate toward in their explorations of guiding questions. Equally important, they offer valuable coaching opportunities before students experience the responsibilities and independence of book groups. Near the end of whole-class novel study, teachers can begin reflecting on sub-questions that emerged from the exploration of a whole-class novel. These questions can then be used to help teachers select literature for book groups.

If we return to *The Great Gatsby* unit from Chapter 4, we can see how the novel also served as an entry point for the discovery of thematic issues students continually revisited and connected with during their reading. Through scrupulous note taking during discussion and a series of personal reflections on classroom activities, Sally and her students uncovered four thematic questions. These themes vary with different classes, but for one particular class, the recurring thematic questions were:

1. What will be our human legacy?
2. What does it mean to be truthful?
3. Who and what determines success?
4. Is what we show the world more important in our success than our inner selves?

From that list of recurring questions, she chose four culturally or socially relevant titles:

1. What will be our human legacy? *Fast Food Nation: The Dark Side of the All-American Meal* by Eric Schlosser (2001)
2. What does it mean to be truthful? *Native Son* by Richard Wright (1940/1996)
3. Who and what determine success? *The Joy Luck Club* by Amy Tan (1989)
4. Is what we show the world more important in our success? *The Things They Carried: A Work of Fiction* by Tim O'Brien (1990)

Each title offered students a different perspective on some of the themes they explored while reading *The Great Gatsby*. Equally important, each genre novel, short story, or nonfiction work offered students a different kind of reading experience.

INVOLVING FAMILIES IN BOOK GROUPS

We understand the limitations some teachers face in getting books into their classrooms. Although we have worked in schools that dealt with extreme deficits, we found that the simple act of asking for help in a trusting and unassuming way helped us get incredible results. After reading all of the texts that will be offered as group reading choices, teachers can use a modified permission slip format to communicate guidelines and needs with parents. We felt it was important to construct a permission slip informed by these two critical assumptions:

1. Parents or guardians want to be invited into the reading lives of their children.
2. Parents or guardians can be trusted to help nurture the adolescents in our classrooms, even though they are busy.

We used this permission slip to help solicit extra copies of texts, communicate with parents about the books and themes, and gain permission for students to read chosen books. Figure 5.1 provides an example of a permission slip we've used.

We need to encourage thoughtful dialogue about texts in our classrooms and with the families of our students. We see the permission slip as a valid

Figure 5.1 Example of a Permission Request to Parents

Dear Parents and Guardians,

Thank you for helping this year with our 9/10 reading workshop. We appreciate all the initial book donations and welcome future donations to our classroom library. We also especially thank those parents who have brought in extra copies of class texts so we can ensure each student can take a text home and write in it! This reading cycle, we will be exploring the following texts and guiding questions. As always, you are welcome to read and discuss with us (seminar days are Fridays):

1. What will be our human legacy? *Fast Food Nation: The Dark Side of the All-American Meal* by Eric Schlosser (2001)
2. What does it mean to be truthful? *Native Son* by Richard Wright (1940/1996)
3. Who and what determine success? *The Joy Luck Club* by Amy Tan (1989)
4. Is what we show the world more important in our success? *The Things They Carried: A Work of Fiction* by Tim O'Brien (1990)

Please discuss these guiding questions with your child and help him or her choose two book choices that are appropriate and potentially engaging. If none of these choices are acceptable, please call us so that we can further discuss the issue. Please write your child's top two choices and sign below. If we do not have a permission slip on file, your child will not be able to begin reading.

Sincerely,
The 9/10 English Team

method of beginning the conversation. We want to encourage young people to talk with the adults in their lives about these big questions; this further strengthens the bond families feel with the educational lives of teens. Permission slips can serve as invitations for parents to read alongside their child, participate in dialogues in or outside of class about the books, or even (as some of our students' parents have) form adult book groups around the novels. Because the permission slips invited them into our classrooms, several parents, grandparents, or guardians visited on random days, sat with their children in book groups, and participated in discussions.

Even with permission slips and dialogues with parents or guardians, some families simply do not have the personal capital to purchase these books. In our situation, we did not have a library in our school, but we did work closely with our students' neighborhood and main public libraries. Several weeks in advance, we provided librarians and parents with our booklists and they helped us create class collections. We supplemented these collections with discounted titles from local used and new bookstores. We found that the people in our school and communities were ecstatic about our book groups and spent many hours tracking down books for our students, settling fines with them for overdue library books, renewing library cards, and dialoguing with us about the texts. We encourage our audience to reach out to parents, public libraries, and local bookstores.

INTRODUCING BOOK CHOICES AND BOOK GROUPS TO STUDENTS

When introducing book choices, it often works best to bring several copies of the listed texts to class. We use a variance of what Janet Allen (2000) calls a *book pass* to get students involved in identifying one of these texts to read. This helps students to focus their characterization of a book, without simply judging by the cover. We organize students into eight small groups (two groups for each title) and put stacks of the same titles at the center of each group. We ask students to take a book and begin reading on any page they chose. They can read out loud to the group or silently to themselves. Afterward, they discuss briefly what they read with the group. Then, they close the book, inspect the cover and read the inside flap or back cover. Finally, they jot down their notes and rate the book on a scale of 1 to 10 for their own purposes. We then ask them to move to the next set of books and repeat the process. Once they have completed all the stations, they sit down and mark their top three choices. These are the books they will dialogue with their parents about reading. Each student chooses their top two texts with the input of a parent or guardian.

After students choose their texts and bring back their completed permission slips, they can be organized into groups. Sometimes, many students will choose the same book, which is fine, so we would have two groups for one novel.

BOOK GROUPS IN ACTION

On the first day of group meeting, the students meet only briefly. At the center of their tables are the copies of extra texts, a manila folder with a calendar stapled to one side, and a list of possible reading responses on the other side. Students work together to assess how much time they have to read the text, how much they can count on each group member being able to read every evening, and what kinds of assignments are tied to the readings. Planning together helps students to build trust in each other, feel trusted and capable in their small reading groups, and hold each other accountable for the requirements. We've found that students not only rise to these standards, but they often take pride in the responsibilities they take in book groups.

Homework and Class Work During Book Groups

Each evening, students read their agreed upon number of pages and choose one response to complete for their book group meetings. These responses span a wide range of representations. Some students create fan pages, blogs, or Facebook accounts as if they were characters in the books. Other students write letters to and from characters, create artistic responses (collage, cartoon, drawing, and three-dimensional displays of scenes, characters, settings, or plots and conflicts), or build ongoing websites for their books. They also get involved in letter-writing campaigns or online petitions as responses to books that have political ties. For example, after reading *They Poured Fire on Us From the Sky: The True Story of Three Lost Boys from Sudan* (Deng, Deng, Ajak, & Bernstein, 2006), some students joined a letter-writing campaign on behalf of lost boys and girls who were in desperate need of assistance in America, and others worked on letters on behalf of those still suffering in war-torn countries everywhere.

We've created our lists of possible response choices as we observe our students' reading patterns over the years. As they evolve due to new technology, different types of print, and social media, so do our lists. We allow our students to teach us about the possibilities for reading responses that are both print- and nonprint-based. We believe this is the only way to honor our students' multiple literacies *and* trust them to be our teachers as well.

What Does a Book Group Meeting Look Like?

On meeting days, students share their reading responses and, as they are sharing, their other group members write discussion questions based on the sharing. For example, if one student shares a series of still photographs that she believes relate to the text, another student, while she is sharing, might write the question: How do the author's clues help us imagine a text more accurately? Or why did you choose this photo to represent that particular character? Questions offer teacher observers material for focused mini-lessons, coaching, and large group facilitation.

Closure and Feedback for Book Groups

At the close of the book group meeting, students place their homework in the folder and leave it on the group table. The teacher then collects the folders and gives focused feedback on the assignments and the discussion she witnessed within the group. For example, if the text were *The House on Mango Street* (Cisneros, 1991), this focused feedback might look something like this:

I really enjoyed the time I spent with your group today. Your discussion of Esperanza's social and cultural pressures provided me with a whole new way of thinking about the novel. I wonder if you've seen any characters similar to Esperanza anywhere else in your lives (movies, music, television, other novels, etc.)? I'm also wondering what your strategies are for getting full group participation in the discussion. Do you think there is anything you could do as a group to encourage quieter members to talk more? How might you invite them into the conversation?

At the next book group meeting, the students exchange their assignments with one another and read over the feedback together. They then discuss the posed questions and write a short response letter to the teacher. This helps strengthen their collaboration and problem-solving skills while continuing the dialogue between groups and the teacher.

WHOLE-CLASS LEARNING DURING BOOK GROUP CYCLES

If a teacher sees a certain pattern emerging in many of the book group discussions, it might be beneficial to bring the whole class together to teach a structured mini-lesson or conduct a seminar on that topic. A pattern might be related to students perpetually summarizing a text in book groups rather than analyzing certain pieces. It could also be related to certain students dominating conversations and not working toward equitable discussions. Both of these examples can be easily remedied through mini-lessons and practice.

The mini-lesson introduces a new concept or way to engage with a text, discussion, or group of peers, and then the book groups can serve as platforms for students to participate in an experience relating to this new skill (guided practice). As the book groups work, the teacher monitors the groups' application and understanding of the mini-lesson's content, and coaches along the way. It may take several meetings before students feel comfortable or exhibit growth in a particular area, but it is with these experiences and the safe and trusting environment of the small group that students will be more likely to take risks and push their own personal boundaries.

Student-led seminars also allow students to learn about texts outside their book groups and further expand their learning. Once or twice per week, the teacher can ask each group to write one universal thematic question that relates to its text on a large sheet of paper. The group then posts that paper at the front of the room to signal their discussion has ended. Usually, students finish their discussions within about 20 minutes. Next, the class assembles in a large group seminar and explores the questions posed by the different groups. (For a refresher on student-led seminar, refer to Chapter 4.) This offers students an opportunity to share ideas, connect texts across time and space, and explore universal themes, characters, or plots. In these macro discussions, students take on the role of experts, explaining and teaching their peers about the details of the books. Big questions connect to textual details, and students come to see themselves and their peers as scholars. They learn to trust the intelligence and authority of the classroom learning community.

FINAL THOUGHTS

Teachers need to spend a considerable amount of time asking themselves what students experience in their classrooms. Teachers also have to remember that adolescents may not be the most respectful, empathetic, responsible, or engaged students. However, it's important to realize that students have the capacity to be all of those things. Moreover, teachers can provide students with experiences that might tap into respect, empathy, responsibility, and engagement, then offer feedback and coaching that helps them learn *how* to interact with others in authentic and personally beneficial ways. Part of this work comes from preparing an environment that has clear and consistent expectations for readers, offers them ways to prove their resilience and independence, and provides them with enough coaching and dialogue so they can be successful in these spaces.

Keep in mind that book groups won't always be successful. Deciding after students are unsuccessful one time with a book group to return to rows and worksheets is sending them the message that students are somehow not deserving of the experiences that good readers benefit from. Teachers cannot foster lifelong reading if they decide superficially that students cannot be trusted to be lifelong readers. Figure 5.2 shows some common problems in book groups and how we remedy them.

Book groups are a great way to prepare students for the independent reading they will do as a part of the I Choose, You Choose curriculum. By beginning with a whole-class text, then moving into book groups, and finally independent reading, teachers can offer a path by which students can be successful with their own independence. Gradually, observe their patterns and what they gravitate toward as individuals; offer them choices within the classroom and plenty of opportunities to reflect on the guiding questions that intrigue them through whole-class novels and book groups. Finally, offer them an opportunity to try out their new understandings of themselves and one another in independent reading. These methods quietly nudge them further from the teacher, so they can begin *doing* the act of reading *alone*.

Figure 5.2. Possible Problems and Solutions in Book Groups

Problem	Solution
Students are unprepared for the discussion	Have the group take a few minutes to prepare some discussion questions for their group. It is best if they also answer these questions when they prepare them—this helps focus minds on the text itself. Students can also pull quotations they liked, draw pictures of inspiring scenes, or compose a brief character sketch. This should last about 5 minutes, to refocus the group.
Certain members dominate the discussion	If this is occurring with several groups, a larger mini-lesson could be useful. It's necessary to model a discussion that is unproductive and have the students discuss its issues and compare it to a productive discussion. This can be done by selecting groups to role play each side. The end of the lesson can be a strategy session for students in individual groups. Ask them if they'd like to create roles for themselves, or keep time. Let the decisions be up to them, but keep a close watch to help them facilitate their new goals.
Hitchhikers (students who don't talk at all, but use other students' work to help get by)	It is very important in these instances to talk with the student yourself privately. There could be a variety of reasons for a student who is not completing work or not talking in the group. If it's a group dynamic, try to bring the group together for a civil discussion. If it's a problem relating to reading levels, work individually with that student on some key skills (Kylene Beers's book *When Kids Can't Read: What Teachers Can Do* [2002] offers many sound ideas for countering this issue). If it's a problem outside of school, work with the student and his or her family to alleviate some of the stress. Sometimes a compromise is necessary.
Cross-Talkers	Cross-talkers are students who talk with others who are not in their groups during the discussions. The best remedy for cross-talking is spacing the groups far enough apart so that each group feels somewhat separate from the rest. This, however, is only a Band-Aid to a problem. Working with the entire class to respect the workspace of others is an essential component in alleviating cross-talking.

Extend Your Thinking

If you've never tried book groups or tried and been unsuccessful, now is the chance to really plan them for your classes. Begin by thinking about the whole-class text you may have chosen for Chapter 4.

1. What were some of the overarching questions students revisited several times during that reading cycle?
2. What are some of the ideas you believe your students are interested in from your observations of them?
3. From these answers, jot down 4 to 5 guiding questions for book groups.
4. Now, select 4 to 5 novels from a diversity of authors and genres that you believe fit with these questions. These novels should also address the range of readers in your classroom, from below-grade level to on-grade level and above.

After you've selected your guiding questions and books, think about how you will acquire all of these books for students.

1. Are you in a situation where students can purchase them?
2. If so, how much time will they need to get the books into their hands? Do you need a permission slip, similar to ours, that helps solicit parental support and approval? If so, when should you send that out?

Now that you have a plan of action, it's necessary to think about what students need from you to be successful.

1. What kinds of mini-lessons will they need initially to be able to respectfully and attentively engage in these groups?
2. How can you ensure that they prepare for each session?
3. How can you extend learning past the small book group?

It's important to remember that, even though it has many benefits for adolescents, group work is often difficult to enact in a classroom without some problems. Once again, we remind you to keep your observation journal handy so you can record any missteps and how you might alleviate them now or the next time you set up the groups. It's through these observational journals that we learn reflective teaching practice and become better each time we revisit a method.

CHAPTER 6

Trust Me! I Can Choose
Valorizing the High School Reader
Through Independent Reading

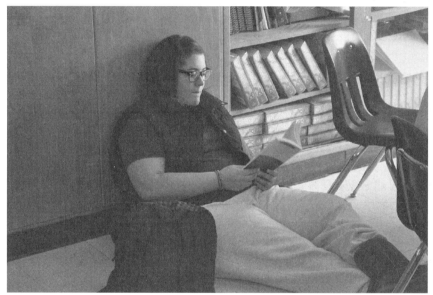

Photo by Michael Smyth

THE ULTIMATE GOAL OF our I Choose, You Choose curriculum is to help adolescents become independent and voracious readers: people who know how to find the answers they need from a wide range of literature, who can discuss their findings, and use these dialogues to further their explorations. We know this is what great readers do, and we know how powerful talking about reading is in adulthood. In *The Reading Zone* (2007), Nancie Atwell admonishes the state of high school reading when she says:

> The sheer waste of time, not to mention opportunity, is beyond lamentable. Young adults are trying to make sense of adulthood—it is *really* just around the corner now—but their schools too often engage them in a version of reading that's so limiting *and* demanding, so bereft of intentionality or personal meaning, that what they learn is to forgo pleasure reading and its satisfactions and, for 4 years, "do English." (p. 107)

We agree with Atwell and believe that the version of reading she describes is deeply tied to notions of achievement. The leadership in many schools and districts believe that such instructional practices prepare students for college level reading, for the SAT and ACT, and, of course, for any state mandated testing during high school. Abandoning independent reading as a way of preparing students for their futures is misguided. Adolescents, similar to adults, have to learn how to use reading for independent purposes in order for it to be relevant in their lives.

Another purpose for independent reading resides in helping students become empowered. When reading in small groups, large groups, or independently, students learn how to navigate complexity, which ultimately helps to build their senses of self. This is what Noddings (1992) describes as confirmation: "When we confirm someone, we spot a better self and encourage its development" (p. 25). We know that confirmation happens in various forms throughout the curriculum, but it truly unfolds during independent reading. During the first few segments of the curriculum, we work toward a deep trusting relationship with students, one that allows us to confirm students on their reading paths during independent reading. This is what Maria Montessori (1948/1992) denotes as valorizing the adolescent. Margaret Loeffler (2003) writes that Montessori's definition of valorization is a process of "integrating a new and more mature personal identity with a sense of being capable of succeeding in life through his or her own efforts" (p. 3). We believe that independent reading, especially in high school classrooms, is an opportunity for teachers to confirm young people during this valorization.

SCAFFOLDING THE INDEPENDENT READING EXPERIENCE

Throughout the independent reading unit, we work behind the scenes to help students be successful at generating independent reading lists, dialoguing with parents, adding or deleting books from their lists, and working through the difficult parts of texts. There are several ways teachers can implement the necessary scaffolding for these experiences.

Using Unifying Elements to Generate Reading Possibilities

The first step in setting up independent reading is to ask students to find an area in which they want to submerge themselves; this helps provide the motivation they need to embrace independent reading. To help get them started, we use an exercise similar to the one that follows. Here we invite readers to experiment with this exercise and dig deeper into their own reading interests.

1. Come up with three lists of the following: five topics you would like to know more about, people you admire, and authors you haven't gotten around to reading.
2. For one of the lists, write for 2 minutes about why you're curious or passionate about it.
3. Articulate a unifying element that can bring a set of books together for you to help you explore a topic, person, or author. In what area can you broaden your knowledge through reading?
4. List all the experts you know (or know about) who could help you generate a list of 10 to 20 books that would deepen your understanding of your unifying element.
5. Call or email your experts to enlist their help in generating an independent reading list. Talk to anyone you know who loves to read—from librarians and booksellers, to an aunt or a neighbor, to a former colleague or college roommate.

Our students choose detective novels, romance, how-to and construction manuals, and novels exploring race, culture, or ethnicity. Figure 6.1 shows some of the unifying elements our students have chosen in the past. Our job is to confirm them in these interests. It is during independent reading that teacher-student trust is truly tested; here, teachers can and should help students join the reading community outside the classroom.

Helping Students Find Reading Experts

Librarians love to help people choose books. And it's their professional responsibility. Before you begin the independent reading cycle, call the local public library in your area and talk with a librarian before sending your students out to them. Librarians should know that students have your support as well as your trust to read what interests them.

In addition, contact your local independent bookstores. Give them notice that the teenagers are coming, but also ask them if they would consider providing "book talks" for your classes or if they have authors visiting that students can go and listen to. Independent bookstores often have very high levels of customer service to help them compete with the chain stores. If your community has only large chain bookstores, the bookstore may just want to get a list of the books you're requiring. Ask to speak with a manager who can recommend employees who are skilled at recommending books to teenagers.

Figure 6.1. Sampling of Unifying Elements Chosen by Students

Authors
Latino/Hispanic writers
Puerto Rican American writers

Themes
African American men and women
Asian American authors
friendship stories
finding one's self
characters suffering from drug addictions
books about basketball
personal finance

Genres & Geographical Areas
American literature
Classic British literature
Japanese literature
Russian literature
Caribbean literature
Autobiography/memoir
Eastern philosophy
Self-improvement

Online searches can provide algorithmic advice. In other words, sites like Amazon.com have honed their programs so that if a student clicks on one book within a genre, he or she will be directed to try out other books that may be of interest. These types of searches are not perfect, but can be useful, especially if a student does not have ready access to a public librarian or bookseller.

Creating the Book Lists

Often, the cover of a text can tell readers a few things about its content. Most readers have a distinct process for selecting books, which we try to emulate for student practice in our classrooms. Students should read the backs of books, listen to what others say about them, and review online summaries. Synthesizing this material, they generate a three- to five-sentence blurb about each book that will help you guide them in their choices and serve as a reminder to them later about each book on their list. Here are our guidelines for constructing lists:

- *Determine the availability of each book.* By knowing ahead of time how many copies of a book are available at the library or whether there tends to be a waiting list for a popular title, students can plan accordingly.
- *Choose twice as many books as you think you can read.* This links directly to the previous point. Often, students cannot find the books they're looking for, so having a larger number than they can read means that they have options.
- *Write a justification for why you want to focus on your unifying element.* We love this part. Students often surprise us with why they want to read a certain set of books. This helps us, as teachers, to "listen carefully" to what our students tell us, so that we can better understand what they are "trying to become" through reading (Noddings, 1992, p. 25). For example, Chris, who had rarely finished a required novel for an English class, submitted his list of books and included titles on money management and self-help. In his justification section, he explained that he had been helping his family with their bills by working, and he hoped to learn financial responsibility so that he could continue to provide for his family. He read every single book on his list, logging in the advice that he received, and writing reflectively about how he could use that information to help him in his job.

Using Dialogue to Collaborate Around Student Lists

Geneva Gay (2002) writes that culturally responsive teachers have a deep understanding of what she terms "culturally responsive caring" (p. 109). Gay reminds us that such teachers must have a vast and deep understanding of their students' cultural backgrounds and how their personal interests may be tied to culture. Nevertheless, she points out that this is not a passive form of caring; it is not enough to simply know and understand a student's culture. Instead, culturally responsive caring in a classroom is "action oriented in that it demonstrates high expectations and uses imaginative strategies to ensure academic success for ethnically diverse students" (Gay, 2002, p. 110). We believe dialogue helps us become better and more responsive teachers.

When implementing independent reading, teachers need to articulate their criteria for lists, but also invite students into the dialogue about their personal reading. Otherwise, independent reading can take the shape of assigned reading. To do this, teachers can focus on helping all students choose lists with appropriate rigor and depth: those that adhere to their unifying element (which is often tied to their lived experiences) and are suitable for their ability to demonstrate mastery of literary standards. Remember that even though a book list might look great in the beginning, a reader grows weary if it doesn't offer what it initially promised. Teachers should be ready to constantly enter this dialogue. Understanding reader weariness and knowing when it is appropriate for students to swap out books from their lists is important. We highlight this dialogue best through the following scenarios.

Daniel the Existentialist. Daniel submitted a list with the unifying element "books about existentialism." His list included Camus's *The Stranger* (1942/1988), *The Plague* (1947/1991), all of Kafka's works, and several Sartre plays, including *No Exit* (1948/1989). His justification read, "The world is a dark place." We had attended several team meetings in which we learned that Daniel had a history of depression. Alarm bells about teen suicide went off when we saw his list, so we met with him. We asked him to expand on his concept of the world as a dark place. Daniel told us that he felt these books would help him understand philosophically how humans have managed depression. He also spoke about how he found his own dark take on the world to be funny—that irony and cynicism were how he entertained himself.

We challenged him to track his observations about representations of cynicism in his journal and seek out friends and community members whom he admires but might not share his worldview. We asked him to see what books they've read that broadened their perspectives. Daniel's final list included Ralph Ellison's *Invisible Man* (1953/1995), short stories by F. Scott Fitzgerald, and poetry by Pablo Neruda and Saul Williams. He did not revise his unifying element; instead, through dialogue, we came to a better understanding of his interests.

Laura the Boundless. Laura, a young woman who consistently pushed the boundaries of appropriateness in attire, language, and reading material, submitted a list with titles that were so smutty, we blushed just reading them. The tamer novels included *G-Spot: An Urban Erotic Tale* by Noire (2006) and *Whore* by Tanika Lynch (2006). As teachers, we have practice in defending books with sexually explicit scenes such as in Souljah's *The Coldest Winter Ever* (1999/2006), but were we prepared to allow our students to read erotica in a high school English class? *Getting Buck Wild* (2003) and *Chocolate Flava* (2004) by Zane are examples of an emerging genre called *eroticanoir*, and the experts some of our students consulted in their communities enjoyed reading these works; we knew further conversation was necessary. We knew we needed to understand Laura's purpose for reading before we moved forward, but we also understood that some of this discussion was beyond the scope of our roles as her teachers. We knew she could benefit from a frank discussion with a parent. We believed it wasn't our place to judge, but to help her find a variety of perspectives.

We asked Laura to read the list aloud to her mother, and offered to be present when she did. In response, Laura asked what she was allowed to read. What she was allowed to read, according to us, was up to her parents, but we wanted to know why she wanted to read these titles. Was she curious about sex? Was she trying to understand how to gain attention of the opposite sex? Were these lived experiences for her that she wanted some perspective about? Some teenagers like Laura are unable or afraid to articulate these goals, so we have to spend more and more time dialoguing with them, and help them reflect on and revise their lists as they begin to understand what they want.

Because Laura was struggling with her purpose, we decided instead to take a step back and look at language and, in turn, how literature that was once controversial in schools becomes classic. We thought this approach might help Laura get to the heart of her purpose. We directed her to research several banned book lists to find books that included language that had once been forbidden, but that had entered the realm of classics. Her final list included some of her original titles and new titles such as D. H. Lawrence's *Lady Chatterley's Lover* (1928/2011), and Ntozake Shange's *For Colored Girls Who Have Considered Suicide When the Rainbow's Not Enuf* (1975/1997). We thought that her new list showed an interest not necessarily in sex, but in relationships, and how women are valued in this context. So, even though Laura couldn't articulate it, the process and the product helped her reach a personal reading goal. In the end, she had a list that her parents approved of and one that allowed her to expand her reading repertoire.

Finally, we encouraged her to explore scholarly writing about explicit literature on her final exam (explained below), learned with her about recent scholarship on urban lit, which explored many of the same questions we had. This co-exploration of literature, family values, and contemporary scholarship engaged Laura directly in the controversy, empowering her to make her own decisions about literature and building trust further among us.

Negotiating Controversial Book Selections. Teachers always want to know what we do when a student submits "inappropriate" titles on their initial list. Although we've discussed some of our reactions in our review of

Laura's list development, we believe it is important to address this subject further with high school reading. Teachers must acknowledge student rights to wonder and know through reading; teachers must also demonstrate high expectations—expectations that allow students to pursue their own growth. Each teacher needs to assess his or her comfort level with discussing matters of sexual explicitness with students and parents, understand district and school guidelines, and to juggle all of this with student learning needs.

Acknowledging students' rights while keeping teacher expectations for learning high requires teachers to be strategic and imaginative. When one of our female students, Brittany, presented us with an independent reading list that included *Chocolate Flava* by Zane (2004), *The Coldest Winter Ever* by Sister Souljah (1999/2006), and *The Pink Palace* by Marlon McCaulsky (2008), we were ready with an action-oriented approach.

We began by asking her to talk in more detail about her interest in these novels. We then pursued a discussion about how these novels might provide answers she seeks to questions she has. After listening to her reasoning, we offered additional novels that we believed would further challenge the roles of African American women in these books and offer her a more rounded perspective. We compromised with Brittany in her final booklist; she read some of the novels we suggested and some of the original list (with parental permission).

We must own that as her White teachers, it is our job to help Brittany find women in her community who can help broaden her understanding of her experiences. We asked her to discuss her list with other women she knows or we know, and add titles that they might offer. Through this, we modeled for her how adults can work together, even if they are from vastly different backgrounds, for the benefit of a child.

In addition, teachers must remember that, although high school students are very close to adulthood and, rightfully, have a multitude of questions regarding their roles as men or women in the adult world, they are still teenagers. As such, teachers also have to seek assistance from their parents in helping them select their literature. A teacher's role is to guide and mentor, not parent. So, we encouraged Brittany to share this list with her parents (and offered to be present to help her through), in order for her to gain assistance in building the list.

We also know from the thousands of students we've taught, that some share more with their teachers than their parents. Sometimes, if parents just saw the titles their children wanted to read, it would offer them opportunities to parent, without feeling like they were prying into a teenager's life. Often, parents are just seeking the right time to dialogue with their children, but teenagers can make this difficult. As teachers, we need to support parent-student dialogues in every way possible. This is a complicated issue because students need us to trust them and parents need to trust us with their children. However, we advocate sharing lists with parents because we believe it increases opportunities for dialogue among the three parties. Because of this, we have entered into conversations with parents about literature that might make some teachers nervous, but there is always an excellent outcome—students have titles they want to read and parents are satisfied. Real education is rarely comfortable, but through dialogue with students and parents, teachers can be pro-active mediators rather than fearful reacters. Often, as in both of the above cases, parents are somewhat shocked by the titles their teenage readers might gravitate toward. Nevertheless, it is the experience of working through this discomfort together that helps us to nurture trust with readers inside and outside of our classrooms. Teachers can play the role of mediator here by encouraging dialogue and offering a series of titles for both parties to consider. Patience is important as well, as families work together to try and understand one another's perspectives. Remember, many teenagers have stopped talking with parents as freely as they did as children. If approached as trust-building opportunities, discussions about literature can be spaces for vital, mature family conversations to begin.

In this process, we use dialogue to teach adolescents how to stand up for their reading choices. Throughout Brittany's life she will often find that, in order to read what she wishes, she might have to defend her choices to her friends, her colleagues, her children, and others. Teachers can help students learn how to defend their choices by first letting them choose what they want to read, and then showing them how to present and read it consciously. This process lets students know that one person or piece of literature does not hold all the answers. Instead, human beings form perspectives from multiple interactions with one another, with literature, and through experience.

Students Who Don't Make a List. Some students don't do the homework, have no idea how to contact a reading expert, and are unprepared. Surprised? Don't be—even after all of these steps, not all students are dying to dedicate their time to independently reading a self-selected set of books. But that doesn't mean that they can't still be successful. We have a fallback list and a unifying element based on the whole-class novels we'll be reading that year (see Figure 6.2). Teachers can create their own list based on what they know about students and curriculum.

Sometimes, students have not had opportunities to discover what they like to read, so we have to engage them in talk about what they *like* in general. For example, Heather, the 1st-year teacher we discussed in Chapter 1, was a nonreader when she entered her English Education program. More

Figure 6.2. Unifying Element and Corresponding Books for Reluctant Readers

Unifying element: narrators who have literal or figurative alter egos

Corresponding Books
Ten Little Indians by Sherman Alexie (2003)
Things Fall Apart by Chinua Achebe (1958/1994)
Stolen by Lucy Christopher (2010)
Frankenstein by Mary Shelley (1818/1995)
The Murder of Roger Ackroyd: A Hercule Poirot Mystery by Agatha Christie
     (1927/2011)
Cut by Patricia McCormick (2000/2011)
The Strange Case of Dr. Jekyll and Mr. Hyde by R.L. Stevenson (1886/1991)
Ceremony by Leslie Marmon Silko (1977/1986)
White Boy Shuffle by Paul Beatty (1996/2001)
Luna by Julie Ann Peters (2006)

This piece is the reality of the classroom. We wish that every student, and almost all do, came up with their own list, but that is not the case. These processes take time, *and* we have to hold students responsible for reading. This does not mean, however, that the dialogue is over. If a student doesn't choose a list for herself, we don't just assign it and move on; note, for example, the amount of time spent working with Laura, Daniel, and Brittany.

specifically, she was an academic reader. She always read everything for class in order to excel academically, but she had no desire to read independently. Frankly, she thought she was a slow reader, and that often deterred her. Initially, it was difficult to tap into her likes and dislikes, but as Sally got to know her, it was clear she liked movies with suspense, complicated characters, action, and a romantic subplot. Even though she is a very capable reader, Sally recommended the young adult novel *The Hunger Games* by Suzanne Collins (2008). Heather read it in a matter of days. From there, she picked up books with similar plot lines, both young adult and adult books, and expanded her reading. She also grew more confident in her academic reading as she began to read more for pleasure.

   This process, however, took time. Heather returned several books to Sally that she had started and stopped. She also finished a few that she felt unimpressed by. It was through these false starts, however, that Sally finally helped her find a niche. Heather needed the conversations with a reading mentor about failed attempts to help guide her in future choices. We engaged in this process endlessly with our high school students; it was not about the fact that a student may have abandoned a text or not even started it, but more about the reasoning behind their decisions. When teachers unlock these conversations, they can better ensure that the next reading might be closer to the perfect fit.

USING TRUST PRACTICES TO SET THE FOUNDATION FOR INDEPENDENT READING

The goal of independent reading is for all students to develop a newfound expertise in an area of their choice, based on their interests. They also receive substantial guided practice in what educators call *lifelong learning,* or the ability to use knowledge and understanding gained from a variety of life experiences (reading, writing, listening, speaking, viewing) to further their chosen academic and personal paths with the goal of continuing these habits into adulthood. Simply by talking about books, picking them off a shelf, sitting down to read them, and writing thoughtfully about what they've learned when they've finished, students develop this crucial capacity. The students also explore individual scholarship—focusing on a single area (again, that they've chosen), and deepening their knowledge about it. To achieve these goals, however, students must feel trusted by their reading communities in- and outside of school. Teachers can set up this foundation by enacting several core trust practices at the beginning of independent reading.

Affirming Trust

Drawing on the lessons students have learned in their book groups, we offer students a scaffolded independent reading experience that affirms our trust in them as readers *and* situates them in an environment in which they can succeed with independent reading. There are several guidelines to our independent reading cycle that help us prepare an environment for student success. We don't want students walking away from this exercise believing that they failed to find the literature they needed.

Building a Unit with Dialogue

Building dialogue with students and offering them the opportunity to contribute to their own classroom experience further builds trust and student buy-in. We start by distributing a draft of independent reading guidelines to the students. The guidelines detail the commitments the teacher and students must make to ensure successful independent reading. Students then review them, add their feedback, and we retype a final version. This collaborative process is essential to use with older students, especially when it is a unit of reading that they are choosing. If they value the opportunity to contribute to their own classroom experience, students take this seriously, especially when they know they can trust the teacher to enact their ideas. Figure 6.3 shows an example of guidelines created for 12th grade.

By using the language of commitment, teachers create a two-way system. We promise to use our professional expertise of literature, teaching, and personal knowledge of our students to help them make good choices, and to help them become stronger, more literate human beings. They, in turn, promise to choose books, get copies of them, to read, and to write. Teachers and students work in collaboration; we make decisions together. Our job from the first introduction of the independent reading lists is to convince them that it's time for them to be self-reliant.

Teaching and Trusting Students to Get Access to Books

The breadth of our experiences as teachers has been in schools where socioeconomics plays a huge role in student access to books. Some students relied on public transportation to get to libraries or bookstores. Others lacked funds to purchase new books and couldn't reliably find used copies. Some families did not use credit cards, so students couldn't order books online. For

Figure 6.3. 12th-Grade Independent Reading Guidelines

Students commit to the following actions:

Generating an independent reading list that centers on a self-chosen unifying
    element.
Getting copies of books in time to begin reading.
Reading for 30 to 45 minutes 5 nights a week.
Using classroom time provided for quiet reading.
Maintaining a *daily* reading log.
Compiling a *weekly* reading log.
Maintaining a record of having mastered district standards.
Completing books in a timely manner.
Writing a recommendation to future readers.

The teacher commits to the following actions:

Providing students with guidance.
Providing students with time to read.
Assessing students' reading logs weekly.
Meeting with students weekly.
Fostering open communication with and among students.
Offering students information and stories about literature.

students with families that offered adequate funds, easy transportation, and credit access, the students themselves often were too busy to hunt down books.

The issue of access is well documented. Neuman and Celano (2001) find that access to books is critical to gaining literacy, and that students in high-poverty areas have less access to books in their communities. Pribesh, Gavigan, and Dickinson (2011) demonstrated that students who attend high-poverty schools are less likely to have access to books through their school libraries. Stephen Krashen (2007) writes that the biggest barrier to reading for high-poverty students is not that they don't want to read, but the lack of access to books. Therefore, we are committed to teaching students not only how to choose books, but how to get them as well.

One of our biggest shortcomings as caring teachers is often that we don't *show* students *how* to navigate the complicated world in which they live. It is much easier to have a school librarian bring books to the classroom, or have the local bookstore hold all the copies at a desk. For some it is easiest to just buy the book for the student and be finished with it. Although these actions are well intentioned, they do not service our students as lifelong readers. In addition, they do not help them develop the self-reliance required to access literature for a variety of contexts in life.

Joe, a student we've mentioned in previous chapters, was going to read *Nickel and Dimed: On (Not) Getting by in America* by Barbara Ehrenreich (2001). He relied on public transportation, worked after school, and did not have the finances to pay for his books. After much pressure from him, his mother finally relented and went to the bookstore on her lunch break to buy the book; however, she came home without it. The next day, Joe came to class and informed us that he did not have the book. He said, "My mom went to buy it, and she says if you all want to pay somebody $14 to talk about life on minimum wage, she'd be happy to come to class and talk." Joe's mother had put us in a difficult position. She had not only refused to buy him the book, but she had made a public statement about it through her refusal. We had an excellent relationship with his mom, and knew that it wasn't that she didn't want him to not read the book, she just didn't want to pay for it. So, we had to show him how to stand up for what he wanted to read.

We got out the bus schedule and found a time when Joe could get to the local library. We then had him use the library website, with our guidance, to find out not only if his branch had the book, but what other local branches also had it. We taught him the hidden tip to our library system that if you call the library directly, it takes less time to get the book than if you place the hold or transfer online. We also taught him that if you call, the library will even hold the book at the front counter on the day you are coming—even send it to the drive-through—if you wish. This simple half-hour lesson took time—time that many teachers profess not to have, but Joe had to make a commitment as well. He spent one of his lunch periods learning how to use the library for his own purposes and with limited time.

Yes, this story comes full circle. Joe got the book from his local library. His mother was absolutely fine with this compromise, and proud of his self-reliance. Joe is now a student at the university where Sally works. He keeps in touch and professes that the library has saved him time and money; it has helped him learn to care for his reading materials better. This simple lesson gave Joe the skills he needed to manage college on a thin budget, control his time and his reading goals, and work around circumstances that limited his access to books. Five years later, we are still happy we spent our lunch period sharing these critical tools with him.

BUILDING A CULTURE OF READING

Helping students navigate the process of accessing literature so they can be trusted to read a text is only one step in lifelong literacy. Building a culture of reading, as Alfred Tatum (2009) describes in his work with at-risk African American male students, provides a space for students to find what matters to them, and what can help them build a "literacy heritage." Part of a teacher's job is to teach her students the tools they'll need to cultivate their own culture of reading. In our work with Joe and countless other students, we know that this process is frustrating and can be time consuming. Sometimes, students are not as receptive as Joe was, but if there is a student who continues to arrive to class with nothing to read, we have done that student a disservice. Throughout the I Choose, You Choose curriculum, teachers must demonstrate a trusting, caring environment. We believe this helps students *want* access to books.

Getting to Work

On the first day of independent reading, we get right down to business. We've prepared for this day throughout the previous reading cycles with whole-class novels and book groups. Students are quite familiar with the expectations for reading, sharing, and collaboration; during each reading cycle (whole class, book groups, and independent reading) students have time to read in class. Likewise, they have already experienced small reading communities, partner work, and student-led seminar, so there are no surprises. We generally take attendance by having the students hold up their books and say their titles aloud. For students who do not have a book, we immediately place a high-interest book from the default list in their hands and move onto the next student.

More than any other question we get about having students read independently during class, teachers and administrators ask, "But what does it look like?" Students read. Quietly. Each brain is engaged in completely separate work. This is good, not something to be feared. Drawing on earlier in-class reading experiences we state that it's time to read, open our own books, invite students to find a comfortable (but not too comfortable) place to sit. We model silent, focused reading and if kids are whispering with one another, we wait for them to quiet. If one student cannot be quiet, then quietly move over and whisper to him or her, "Please be sure to allow other students to read—they'll be upset if we lose our time to read because of you." Trust the students to begin reading, and most often, they will. During reading workshop, we watch the richness of engagement that comes from student choice, and know that our students are on their way to achieving that elusive yet essential pedagogical goal: becoming lifelong learners.

Providing Support Through Daily Check-In

Clearly, teenagers need to trust that you're engaged with them, working along with them. We typically read with students for the first 5 minutes or so of independent reading, setting the tone by modeling our own reading. Often the books we've chosen are those that students have just finished reading and have recommended. This is a fantastic trust-builder. After the students have settled into their reading, we take up our clipboards and make rounds.

We move from student to student, taking care to maintain the studious atmosphere of the class, and quietly checking in and providing support in whichever ways students need us. The goal of checking in is twofold:

1. To document each student's progress with a certain book.
2. To scaffold the reading process for each student.

Because we've gotten to know students as readers in our classrooms, it's easy for us to ask them specific questions that will appeal to them as readers. In the early stages of independent reading, we ask them what they're reading, record the page number, and often just ask, "Any questions?" In the later stages, we ask about characters or use points they've made in their journals to open a quick dialogue with them. A simple question at this phase might be: "I noticed in your journal last night that you seem bothered by some of the main character's actions. Why do you think you feel this way?" Usually, this opens the door for a student to voice his or her opinions about a character, the choices an author makes, and the student's own understanding of right and wrong. This simple question shows a student we are genuinely interested in his or her perspective. It is also strategic because it pushes a student to delve into issues of characterization, tone, and author's purpose without overtly teaching them.

It is highly beneficial if we can dialogue with students each day about their books, but we also must recognize their rights to reading time. Checking in verbally once or twice a week during workshop suffices if a teacher is also collecting weekly journal entries. Nevertheless, both are important. Students will discuss things in face-to-face conversations that they might not focus on in journals and we can use their journals to build our dialogues with them.

Communicating Feedback Through Weekly Journals

Because students are reading different books, we need to trust them to communicate with us. Developing a weekly journal format that allows students to discuss their reading, improve their writing, and attend to district and state standards is crucial to successful independent reading.

We allow students time to write in their journals during class reading time and resist the urge to have them write volumes about their books by considering what our goals are, what we need to know from them, and what skills our students need to work on. With this in mind, we ask students to provide a sentence or two to establish what's going on in the book and to limit their weekly journal writing to no more than two pages. For a reluctant writer, we encourage at least three or four sentences for section (see below). Since we are visually and verbally checking in their reading pace during daily check-ins, we don't need to use journals to be convinced *that* they're reading; we want journals to show us *how* and even *why* students are reading. As students move along in the program, they can often create their own journal format, but teachers can get them started with these sections:

- Reflect (connect to your personal life)
- Analyze (discuss and analyze the author's craft of writing)
- Interpret (connect to larger themes, other texts, and address complexities and nuances—what captures this book's qualities?)
- Evaluate (judge writer's effectiveness and assess the book's various parts—no book is entirely either good or bad—what can it offer to yourself and other readers?)

These categories are taken directly from our state and district standards of writing, and we teach each skill directly during mini-lessons. (For more on demonstrating mastery over standards, see the following section.)

Collecting and grading journals is an essential part of this program, as students need regular feedback. Prior to journal writing, we provide students with a simple 4 x 4 rubric (see Figure 6.4), based on the aforementioned

Figure 6.4. Rubric for Scoring Independent Reading Responses

Area of interaction	4 Excellent	3 Advanced	2 Adequate	1 Needs further coaching
Reflections	The student makes thorough connections to his or her personal life, giving substantial textual evidence to support anecdotal details.	The student makes several connections to his or her personal life, giving examples from the text to support ideas.	The student makes broad connections to his or her life, and supplies surface details from the text as support.	The student can make broad connections with the text.
Analysis	The student discusses author's craft by analyzing his or her use of voice, literary devices, and specific elements of characterization. He or she can substantially support this analysis through specific and detailed textual evidence that builds on previous ideas.	The student discusses author's craft and analyzes his or her use of literary devices. He or she supports this analysis with textual examples.	The student can locate areas of text where the author uses specific literary devices and summarize these areas in relation to the plot.	The student can locate general areas where literary devices occur, and provides general summaries of these sections.
Interpretation	The student thoughtfully and clearly identifies universal themes, archetypal characters, and subtle nuances in the text. He or she can substantially support these connections and build on them to connect to other texts and the text's significance in the "real" world.	The student clearly identifies universal themes, and connects characters and plots to other texts and global events. The student provides clear support for these connections.	The student identifies some themes and connects the text to global or personal events. He or she uses textual support sparingly.	The student can identify major themes in the text.
Evaluation	The student uses all of the above skills to soundly and clearly judge the significance of the work. He or she can thoroughly compare this significance to other texts across time periods. He or she can substantially support these judgments with evidence from all pieces.	The student uses the above skills to judge the significance of the work in its entirety. The student can support this judgment through textual evidence and makes connections to other texts across time periods.	The student can communicate his or her ideas about the effectiveness of the piece. He or she uses supporting textual evidence sparingly.	The student can judge the significance of the work on a personal level.

categories and ask them to glue it to the inside front cover of their notebooks as a reminder of our expectations.

Dean asks students to turn in their journals at the beginning of class on Fridays, and assesses them while the students are reading. Sally staggers her journal collection throughout the week so that she reads one set per evening. We do not provide extensive feedback. Often, we will write a short note to students regarding their books (Atwell, 2007) or note in our planners to speak with them directly about issues in their books. By keeping assessment brief and transparent for teachers and students, we can focus on reading what the students have written, and then take note of students who need the most work during daily check-ins.

Demonstrating Mastery over the Standards

We know that reading great books enhances students' learning, and by having the opportunity to choose their own titles, students read more. The remaining piece of the puzzle, regardless of where you stand on the standards movement, is to bridge the gap between what your district and school expect and what your students are able to demonstrate about their ability to read well. If your district downplays explicit teaching of standards, then you can omit this step. If, however, your students are expected to demonstrate their mastery over the standards, as most of the NCLB generation is, then you might consider creating a bookmark of the benchmarks/standards/skills your students are expected to master. Figure 6.5 is an example of a bookmark we created. The numbers and text in the figure correspond to our district's benchmark skills, which we've organized according to each skill set students are expected to master. Students documented their mastery of the standards in their journals.

Give the bookmarks to students at the beginning of their independent reading and have plenty on hand as the year progresses. Students use the bookmarks as a visual reminder of what standards they're looking for as they read. The bookmarks serve as checklists of the literary tools authors use and the language arts skills students have mastered. For example, students write the page number of the literary element directly on their bookmark and then go back later to show their mastery over it in their journals. Students love the bookmarks for several reasons: as a simple tool to help them with their homework, as a validation that their own hunches about what makes a piece of writing strong are part of the technical vocabulary about literature, and because it helps them to retain the challenging lessons of rhetoric and writing.

FIGURE 6.5. Benchmark Skills Bookmark

Author's Purpose:

5.68: Explain how authors use symbols to create broader meanings.

5.74: Recognize how irony is used in a literary text.

Point of view, mood, and tone:

5.67: Analyze ways in which the author conveys mood and tone through word choice, figurative language, and syntax.

5.75: Analyze the author's use of point of view, mood, and tone.

5.77: Explain ways in which an author develops a point of view and style (e.g., figurative language, sentence structure, and tone), and cite specific examples from the text.

5.81: Evaluate the author's use of point of view in a literary text.

5.85: Evaluate ways authors develop point of view and style to achieve specific rhetorical and aesthetic purposes (e.g., through use of figurative language, irony, tone, diction, imagery, symbolism, and sounds of language), citing specific examples from text to support analysis.

Sound devices:

5.69: Identify sound devices in literary texts.

5.76: Describe the effect of using sound devices in literary texts (e.g., to create rhythm, to appeal to the senses, or to establish mood).

Characterization:

5.70: Compare and contrast an author's use of direct and indirect characterization, and ways in which characters reveal traits about themselves, including dialect, dramatic monologues, and soliloquies.

5.80: Explain how voice and narrator affect the characterization, plot, and credibility.

Setting:

5.71: Analyze the features of setting and their importance in a literary text.

5.79: Analyze the historical, social, and cultural context of setting.

Plot:

5.72: Distinguish how conflicts, parallel plots, and subplots affect the pacing of action in literary text.

5.73: Explain how literary techniques, including foreshadowing and flashback, are used to shape the plot of a literary text.

Themes & Conflict:

5.78: Compare and contrast motivations and reactions of literary characters confronting similar conflicts (e.g., individual versus nature, freedom versus responsibility, individual versus society), using specific examples of characters' thoughts, words, and actions.

5.82: Analyze variations of universal themes in literary texts.

Subgenres:

5.83: Recognize characteristics of subgenres, including satire, parody, and allegory, and explain how choice of genre affects the expression of a theme or topic.

5.86: Recognize and differentiate characteristics of subgenres, including satire, parody, and allegory; and explain how choice of genre affects the expression of theme or topic.

Literary eras & regions:

5.84: Analyze the characteristics of various literary periods and how the issues influenced the writers of those periods.

5.87: Compare and contrast varying characteristics of American, British, world, and multi-cultural literature.

Adapted from Cincinnati Public Schools, *English/Language Arts Resource Binder* (2004)

FORMAL ASSESSMENTS AND INDEPENDENT READING

If students spend time during the year pursuing independent study, then how do we write a final exam? By continuing to empower students and to allow for choice. This is where the unifying element comes in handy. We invite students to take a place at the table of scholars. They have, at the midway point in the year, read at least two or three books within a single genre, by a single author, or about a single theme. We ask students to think of themselves as emerging experts. We take a step back from the immediacy of reading one book, and have them do the following:

1. List characteristics of the books you have read. (These typically include author's style, historical significance, popularity among teens, genre.)
2. Identify defining elements or patterns.
3. Develop a theory about what appears to be true about the unifying element.
4. Find and read a scholarly article that ties to the unifying element.
5. Write an independent scholarship essay that explains your own observations about your unifying element as well as support from the scholarly article.

This is a critical phase in independent reading. It is at this time that students have an opportunity to broaden their perspectives on chosen titles. Equally, it is an opportunity for us to "build toward academic success from a basis of cultural validation and strength" (Gay, 2002, p. 110).

We can look back to our student example, Olivia, who came to us wanting to read a series of novels that deal with modeling. Through our dialogues with Olivia, her mother, and Olivia's chosen community experts, we helped Olivia round out her independent reading list with additional titles that also spoke of African American female identity and struggle, but in a different context than the one she selected. For some students, the discrepancy between these works might be transparent. Reading Toni Morrison, Maya Angelou, or Nikki Giovanni's classic works in the company of former model and fashion designer Kimora Lee Simmons's *Fabulosity: What It Is and How to Get It* (2006), one might immediately understand the commentary or gain new perspective. Nevertheless, it is also entirely possible that a teenager might see each of these texts separately from each other, even though they unifying qualities.

As we've stressed throughout this book, when we push students to become critical about their choices, we must be careful not to judge their interests, but to provide varying points of view on a topic at their disposal so they can learn to read each piece with a critical eye. An age-old issue for women, especially teenagers, is society's definition of beauty. As Olivia's White teachers, we were socialized early into White notions of beauty. We can (and should) try to understand what our African American female students strive for, but we need resources from their communities to help us nurture their forming identities. We have to recognize our limitations here. So, we asked Olivia to use the reading experts who helped build her list and, for the final exam, she returned to these experts to further her understanding.

We (meaning all of us) helped her find a series of scholarly articles on African American women and physical beauty, how the media and advertising portray this, and why these portrayals can be damaging for young people. We did not tell Olivia that what she was reading was bad for her. Instead, we helped her diversify her resources so that she could read to find her answers. For her final exam, Olivia used these articles to write a critique of the modeling industry from the point of view of an African American teenager. She illuminated, for us and her audience, the difficulties she was experiencing in finding a balance between what she believed society wanted and what she wanted or believed was a healthy self-image. Olivia still reads modeling magazines and has a great interest in her external beauty (like many of us, she takes pleasure in these activities), but she understands it critically, which is different from how she began this process.

FINAL THOUGHTS

It is important to celebrate the end of this cycle with students. What they have achieved during their independent reading contributes greatly to their personal growth as teenagers and critical readers. So, we arrange for them to be reflective, but also congratulate them on what they've accomplished. Final projects can include

- compiling an annotated bibliography for future students;
- creating a collage that displays what they loved and learned about their unifying element;
- making a movie trailer about their newfound knowledge;
- scheduling a roundtable discussion with the community experts who have helped them; and
- showing off the results of their readings through a student-taught lesson.

One of the greatest results of the celebration is that these presentations serve as platforms for other students to become interested in the books their classmates have read. Our students are sharing a whole series of books and an entire accumulation of knowledge. We make it special and encourage them to be creative with their final projects by considering the audience of their peers. Often, they trade books and suggest other titles to one another after the presentations (isn't this what great readers do, anyway?). All of this culminates in our final and necessary closing questions for students:

- What is your next reading project going to be?
- Where else can your interests take you?
- How have you been inspired to learn?

Extend Your Thinking

As you can see, a lot of work goes into the independent reading cycle. In this section, we invite you to look back over all of your notes on this book and think more about independent reading with your high school students:

1. Look over your lists of guiding questions and novel choices for your I Choose, You Choose curriculum. How can these cycles work to build the independent reading experience in your classroom?
2. What do you believe your students' hurdles will be in getting books? How will you overcome these hurdles with them?
3. What are your feelings about controversial reading? How will you dialogue with parents about students' choices?
4. Finally, how will the independent reading cycle fit with the standards you are currently working with in your classroom? What types of assessment (formal and informal) could you use to show student understanding of these?

Trust Me! I Can Read
Subverting the Pedagogy of Poverty

A S WE DISCUSS IN the Introduction, we believe that NCLB and *A Nation at Risk: The Imperative for Educational Reform* (National Commission on Excellence in Education, 1983) have together done more to erode trust in the American public school system than any other single force. So what can we do to salvage and rebuild trust, specifically classroom trust practices?

Because scripted curricula and tests push teachers to see students as empty vessels rather than individuals who bring a specific set of knowledge and skills to nurture in the classroom, they no longer trust what students bring to them is valid. To overcome this, they have to re-educate ourselves about the classroom practices that promote resilience, self-reliance, interdependence, and knowledge—that is, a desire to know *more* about a specific subject, topic, or author. These are the practices that trust in the capacity of the human mind.

In the contentious environment of scripted curricula and testing, however, it is not helpful to think of teachers as suffering war heroes and students as the spoils of someone else's war. We need to return to the task at hand: building trusting relationships between teachers, students, and the content that we share. We argue it is the only way to become lifelong readers. We must diffuse the battle and model the same practices inside and outside of our classrooms—knowledge, interdependence, self-reliance, and resilience. In his book *In Praise of Education* (1997) John Goodlad writes that schools with trusting relationships "have such relationships between teachers and pupils in the classrooms, between parents and teachers, and between schools and homes" (p. 136). We must admit, however, that often new teachers must prove their mastery not only within the discussions surrounding their classroom practices, but also with student results, in order to be seen as trustworthy by other teachers, administrators, and parents. Sadly, it is infrequent that teachers enter classrooms or schools where they are already trusted to teach their students effectively.

Our goal must be to develop the talents of all (teachers, students, and administrators) to their fullest. Attaining that goal requires that we expect our school communities to work to the limits of their capabilities, and we trust ourselves as competent stewards for those who are less experienced. As *A Nation at Risk* emphasizes, we should expect schools and teachers to have genuinely high standards rather than minimum ones, and parents to support and encourage their children to make the most of their talents and abilities.

This message of hope, with specific attention to providing equity in our school systems, as well as to promoting high, rigorous standards that will help our students become life learners, aligns with our own sense of what it means to trust that all of our students learn, are literate beings, and have the right and responsibility to read rich, engaging literature throughout their lives. By providing them the opportunities to choose their own books, engage in discussions with their peers and teachers about literature, and write meaningful responses to literature, both formal and informal, we are not only stewards of their literary journeys, but we move beyond *A Nation at Risk's* self-described "act of war"(1983).

RELEARNING HOW TO READ

When we trust books to rekindle the intrinsic motivation students have to learn, inquire, find answers, and ultimately grow, we are going against the system of schooling, which is full of extrinsic rewards such as grades and test scores for students' academic actions. Students who are motivated intrinsically to read have stronger gains in reading ability over a long period of time than students who read for external motivations such as grades or parental pressure (Becker, McElvany, & Kortenbruck, 2010; Retelsdorf, Koller, & Moller, 2011). Because the motivation is external, students work not within the journey but toward the expected product, which is often designed by a teacher. In these situations, open-ended explorations are only literal, and students have trouble delving deeper into a subject if the product doesn't require it. These are the points at which students stop learning for themselves and start learning as a means to an end. To say that books can cure our classroom ills is naive, but to trust that they can spark intrinsic motivation in our students is quite accurate. Throughout this book, we've shown how teachers can counteract this pattern in a high school English classroom.

MAKING THE IMPOSSIBLE MANDATORY IN HIGH SCHOOL ENGLISH CLASSROOMS

Some might say that our methods would never work in a typical high school English classroom, where students don't have intrinsic motivation, and teachers have to assess outcomes. We believe this is cowardice. Teachers can, as we have outlined, design a curriculum that focuses on mastery rather than outcomes—one that taps into adolescents' desire to share with their peers and valorizes the individual by leaving projects open-ended for exploration. Students who have opportunities to master their reading *will* do better on whatever outcome-based assessment confronts them. This is simple because, when students are motivated intrinsically to read, their reading skills will improve (Becker, McElvany, & Kortenbruck, 2010). As teachers, we think this is enough. For administrators, remind them that students who spend more of their free time reading (without any rewards but for their own benefit) do better on the tests, are more likely to be civically involved, and, most importantly engage in reading for life (ACT, 2009; Bradshaw, 2004). It is when we make reading a chore or outcome based that students become disillusioned by books.

Bridging the Gap between Classroom and Systemic Assessments

The remaining piece of the puzzle, regardless of where you stand on the high-stakes testing movement, is to bridge the gap between what types of mastery evidence you have from your classroom observations and what types of mastery evidence your school or district requires. How does what you do in a classroom to show mastery translate to the narrow form of assessment used by your district?

Some teachers can be masters of their content, excellent observers, copious note takers, and great record keepers. They might understand all the cues of students' engagement with the material, have trusting relationships with students, provide various opportunities for all learners to develop and demonstrate mastery, and create an excellent mix of choice and teacher direction in the classroom. By some district and state standards, however, if their students are not performing on the standardized tests, both parties are failing. Any teacher who is doing all of the above pieces well, we argue, also has students doing well on the tests. The key lies in the honest and continuous examination of practices and relationships with students.

Through reflective practice, teachers push themselves to use observations to become better. We would argue that it is impossible for a reflective educator to teach the exact same lesson to five straight classes of different students. Teachers are constantly immersed in the act of revising their instructional approach for the specific students they meet throughout the day. Nevertheless, standardized tests have become part of classroom work as well.

Teachers who know their students well and trust their learning know that many of the factors contributing to success on the tests have to do with factors out of their control, such as nutrition and sleep patterns, as well as factors within their control, such as building confidence and fostering intrinsic motivation. Each of these factors can be affected by race, class, gender, and a whole host of other sociocultural pieces, but, in essence, we are talking about basic human tendencies and needs—the need to sleep, eat, feel confident, and find a purpose in life. However, consider the message that the following paragraph from our state test coordinator's manual sends:

> A student who becomes ill and vomits on her or his test booklet or answer document and is able to continue the test should be given a new test booklet or answer document so that she or he may continue. Later, the student's responses and demographic information must be transcribed into the new answer document, which will be the copy of the test to be scored. The soiled test booklet or answer document should be placed in a ziplock bag with the barcode written on the ziplock bag and returned to the DTC with the unused materials. (Ohio Department of Education, p. 24)

The manual goes on to give explicit directions for students who are unable to continue the test, as deemed by the district. There is extensive language about proper transcription of answers from the soiled booklets and subsequent mandatory testing.) Year after year, the aforementioned paragraph appears in the test coordinator's directions. It illustrates that in the world of testing, the proper completion of a valid test booklet is more important than the welfare of the student, whose performance will be undeniably affected by such an incident.

The most effective and nurturing teachers would be naive to spend time and energy trying to dismantle that system, so teachers have to chip away at it by helping students demystify the tests for themselves. Teaching our students to take a critical approach to high-stakes tests is better than complaining to them about the tests or passively accepting this reality.

Demystifying Assessment

Instead of spending hours doing practice tests leading up to the actual test, you could open the dialogue about the test at the beginning of the year. When you teach students about how to approach a standardized test, you give them lifelong tools for dealing with assessment. Having them repeat practice test after practice test, at best, gives them multiple opportunities to become frustrated and disillusioned with the test and reading.

In our classes, we spent a considerable amount of time discussing the author's purpose. Our students could detect nuances in texts and examine their own relationships with an author through a text. We practiced the same relationship with the standardized tests by asking: Who are the authors of these tests (race, class, gender, profession, etc.)? What do they want from you (specifically)? Why do they want it? This is a practice that yields answers for our students. When they find out who does write these tests and how they formulate the questions, who scores tests, and what the scores are used for, they become conscious consumers of the tests. They are beginning to learn the game and the power of their autonomy. After we begin this dialogue, we move on to talking about specific sample test questions throughout the year.

On days when we discuss irony, we might put a test question up on the board. With their partners, we ask our students to answer our three questions: Who wrote this question? What does this person want from you? Why does he or she want it? After they have discussed these questions with their peers, we ask: Should you give this person what he or she wants? Why or why not? If yes, how do you go about doing that? What are the repercussions of your decision either way? They then go back to their partners and discuss. It is in the midst of the discussion that they, as a community, begin weighing their options with these tests and all of life's assessments.

There is never an assumption that the students can't answer the question, but instead a discussion of whether they will. We dialogue about it, but we trust them to make the choices that make sense to them. We remind them that they have the knowledge the test wants, but it is their choice to play the game or not. We show them how to play by reading into the purpose of the questions, eliminating answers, and identifying certain words that indicate a desired response. These are skills all students should have access to, but what is of utmost importance is the deconstructing dialogue that happens throughout the year regarding the test. This conversation helps our students take control of what is being asked of them from the tests and from the variety of life situations in which they are asked to conform to some kind of standard. We have to teach them, as emerging adults, how to critically navigate all the nuances of assessment in their lives.

We do not do isolated test preparation; our students deserve to spend their class time engaged in activities that push them to evolve as human beings. The most powerful tool we have is what Megan Tschannen-Moran (2004) calls openness—"Engaging in open communication, sharing important information, delegating, sharing decision making, sharing power" (p. 19). This is a simple idea that we've carried out with fidelity. It builds trust with our students. We share with our students the history of the standardized testing movement—both the unfortunate history of racial bias in the test-creation process and the positive role these tests have played in unearthing inequity across schools and districts. We talk about the frequent disconnect between classroom learning and test items. We also share the stories of successful people who did not score well in high school and—perhaps most important—lists of colleges that look beyond standardized test scores when evaluating student applicants. We make explicit to them that the learning they experience in our classes is real. We trust that they can read, and use their reading for their chosen paths. This is part of our daily belief system; by pairing it with rigorous literary instruction and high standards that push them beyond what the district asks, students learn that they can read and learn purposefully.